CRICKET'S GREATEST BATTLES

CRICKET'S GREATEST BATTLES

NASSER HUSSAIN · PETER BAXTER
MIKE BREARLEY

generation PUBLICATIONS

Edited by Phil McNeill

Designed by Robert Kelland

With thanks to Eve Cossins, Mark Crossland, Catherine McNeill, Clare Reeve, Clair Reynolds, Chris Young, Adrian Waddington; to Bob Warde and Gough Warde for supplying the cigarette cards, and to Lara Piercy and Rob Brown at Colour Systems

Special thanks to all the cricketers who contested the battles within these pages

Published by David Crowe and Mark Peacock

First published in Great Britain in 2000 by Generation Publications
9 Holyrood Street, London SE1 2EL

genpub@btinternet.com

Text copyright © Generation Publications

A catalogue record for this title is available from the British Library

ISBN 1 903009 36 7

Production by Mike Powell & Associates (01494 676891)
Origination by Colour Systems Ltd, London
Printed and bound in Italy by Giunti Industrie Grafiche

Page 2: The lucky few in the crowd at the end of the 1963 Lord's Test stage a pitch invasion. Mind your arm, Colin!
Page 3: Brian Lara grimaces as he is hit by a ball from Glenn McGrath during the 1999 battle of Sabina Park
Left: Devon Malcolm rolls South Africa over at The Oval, 1994

Contents

PETER BAXTER

NASSER HUSSAIN

MIKE BREARLEY

A quiet word before the storm

No other team game encompasses such individual battles as cricket. There is the lonely batsman facing a fast bowler with his dander up; the guileful spinner trying to out-think his adversary; the team apparently facing defeat, finding in one person – or perhaps a pair of batsmen or bowlers – the sheer guts or genius to defy a rampant opposition.

These are events and qualities to celebrate, and we hope our team has done them justice in these pages.

The confrontations we've selected span an entire century, from the Yorkshiremen Hirst and Rhodes clawing their way to victory against Australia in 1902, to Steve Waugh's fight to keep the Aussies in the World Cup in 1999.

If anyone had mentioned 'match-fixing' to Wilfred Rhodes, he would probably have thought it was a new way of lighting his pipe. Sadly, those innocent days are gone, and today's international cricketers cannot easily escape the shadow that hangs over the sport they love.

Yet a higher innocence still holds sway, because cricket's greatest battles encapsulate the purest aspect of sport – the duel. In this arena, there is no escape. In sporting terms, it is mortal combat. The moral fibre of each man is examined, not by the lure of a 'bung', but by the heat of the battle.

With all due respect to Pelé, cricket really is the beautiful game. These are a few of its finest moments.

PREFACE

It takes all sorts to make a battle... Stubbornness, quirkiness, savagery – cricket has room for them all

The games within the game

By Mike Brearley

The Holy Grail of every sportsman is perfect psychological balance between spontaneity and control. Such an aim is shared, of course, with people in many areas of life. All creative activity, from teaching children to directing a film, requires this delicate and difficult balancing act. No one can reliably achieve and maintain such an aim, but everyone gets moments when they have intimations of this happy state.

Spontaneity arises from passion, from self-acceptance, from freedom. One paradoxical feature of such an aim is that one can't work at it head-on. One can't achieve spontaneity by earnest endeavour. As the poet writes: *"You praise the great restraint with which they write. I'm with you there of course. They use the snaffle and the bit all right but where's the bloody horse?"*

The sportsman, like the teacher, film director and so

> *'The book's title at once draws attention to a central aspect of sport: that it is a development from, and refinement of, fighting.'*

on, becomes successful by a combination of innate qualities, training and technique; but the hardest quality to put one's finger on, let alone train up, is the strength and freedom of character, the capacity to make full use of one's talents spontaneously. He or she requires courage and endurance; flair and patience; the ability to rise with passion to the occasion, and a certain inner calm. He has to have a sense of when it is best to take risks, when to dig in. He needs to retain confidence even when out of form, but also be open to constructive self-criticism.

He has to be in tune with reality; both external reality – knowing who he's competing against, and the conditions of pitch and time – and internal reality – knowing his limitations without losing touch with his strengths (or vice versa).

Sport represents national and local characteristics. It is

'The sportsman becomes successful by a combination of innate qualities, training and technique; but the hardest quality to put one's finger on, let alone train up, is the strength and freedom of character to make full use of one's talents spontaneously.'

Cricketing warrior: England captain Mike Brearley "joins the crash helmet brigade" on the eve of the 1978 Lord's Test against Pakistan

Cricket – a game of individuals who often prefer to hunt in pairs… Ramadhin & Valentine (above); Hobbs & Sutcliffe (right). Cricketers come in every shape, size and class, from the toff to the working man … Douglas Jardine (right); Wilfred Rhodes & George Hirst (below)

not for nothing that the words of George Hirst to Wilfred Rhodes (1902) – "We'll get 'em in singles, lad" – have become part of folklore in Yorkshire, since they so neatly epitomise the careful, shrewd co-operation of working men in a hard world. Yorkshire grit produces a different breed of sportsmen from those produced by the public school system, or by the more foreign cultures and climates of Barbados or Bangalore.

On occasion, sporting struggles symbolise massive conflicts of history, which have informed life in ways that go far beyond sport. Think of the Bodyline series (1932/3), and its relation to colonialism; or the Test match between South Africa and West Indies in 1995 in the shadow of apartheid which had so recently been dismantled.

But cricket is unique. Of all ball games cricket is one of the slowest, and the longest-lasting. It is probably the only one where a single match can be scheduled for almost a week, at the end of which there may be no winner or loser. This dimension of time means that excitement and adrenalin cannot carry one far, that there is room for ennui (as in life itself), but also for epic struggles, in which the tension gnaws agonisingly as it mounts to a final climax.

The top-class cricketer needs to be dogged; able to endure the longueurs and attritions that are an inevitable part of so long-drawn-out a battle. Pitch conditions change radically, too, even within a single game. A cricketer has to be flexible and resourceful. There is a wide variety of skills. The complete batsman, for instance, is fazed neither by the physical threat posed by an Ambrose or a Donald, nor by the intricate wiles of a Warne or a Muralitharan.

Unlike baseball, cricket permits runs to be scored all

round the wicket, not only in a 90-degree arc, and the ball bounces, veers, lifts, shoots and spins – all variations and sophistications lacking in the cruder American version.

Cricket, like baseball, is a game of individual contests within a team context, unlike football on the one side, or tennis on the other. Hence this book features not only mighty battles between protagonists, but also contests in which one man stands out against all that a team can throw against him.

Cricket also embraces in its fascinating complexity the fact of pairings – stirring partnerships, as between Hobbs and Sutcliffe, or between bowlers hunting in tandem, like Walsh and Ambrose – another fact recognised in this book.

The book's title at once draws attention to a central aspect of sport: that it is a development from, and refinement of, fighting. Some of the greatest cultural achievements of human beings harness the evolutionarily necessary instinct of fighting and defending oneself. Even so sublimated an activity as drama, incidentally, may have derived from contentiousness and war; the word for the metre of Classical Greek drama, 'iambics', derives from the Greek word that means 'throw'. Thus we may imagine the great dramas of psychological conflict and tragedy growing out of the practice of hurling insults at one's enemies rather than rocks or spears – itself a massive development in civilisation.

Cricket, like other sports, calls for martial qualities: courage, aggression, steadfastness, cunning, strength. The all-round ideal combines the all-out passionate aggression of an Allan Donald in his pomp, with the gutsy, never-say-die, backs-to-the-wall obduracy of a Michael Atherton. It includes the unflinching optimism of the underdog – Tendulkar or Lara carrying the fight to the current Australians – and the relentless ambition of his opponents to maintain their supremacy.

All sorts of diverse human qualities may be enlisted in the fight: think of the eccentric antics of Derek Randall, doffing his cap to the mighty Dennis Lillee after marginally evading a bouncer, puzzling the Australians with his provocative and enigmatic quirkiness.

His innings at Melbourne in 1977 is a real-life

'The complete batsman is fazed neither by the physical threat posed by a Donald, nor by the intricate wiles of a Warne or a Muralitharan...'

'If we play well enough, we belittle our achievement by telling ourselves that the opposition are below par, or we have been lucky.'

'This book features not only mighty battles between protagonists, but also contests in which one man stands out against all that a team can throw against him.'

Ian Botham, hero of Headingley '81; Nasser Hussain, hero of Edgbaston '97

instance of Gerry the mouse putting Tom the cat in his place; it doesn't only happen in the cartoons.

Tony Greig (Brisbane 1974/5) also provoked the Australians in his own extrovert fashion. He calculated that whenever Lillee lost his cool and tried to hit the batsman in preference to getting him out he actually bowled worse. So, with remarkable sang-froid, Greig provoked this most aggressive of bowlers into outright personal attack.

At Lord's in 1964 Brian Close used a tactic that was no doubt a new experience for the great West Indian fast bowler Wes Hall, when he defied him in a titanic struggle between these two lasting several hours. At one point not long before the nail-biting end of a wonderful Test match, Close advanced down the pitch towards Hall as if he were a mere medium-pacer. The latter was so disconcerted that he pulled up in delivery stride, unable to believe his eyes; what batsman in

MAURICE LEYLAND

his right mind would advance on him rather than, as more commonly, retreat? (Close used to say that a cricket ball can't hurt you as it's only on you a second.)

'Fast bowling," the Yorkshire batsman Leyland once said in his broad Yorkshire accent, "keeps you honest." There is no escape when you bat against the fastest bowlers. You can't fool yourself for long about your courage, or lack of it. Test cricket is indeed a test – of character as much as of skill and technique.

The more we know, the more we realise how much courage it takes. My old Middlesex opening partner Mike Smith used to tell how, during the TV excerpts from Australia in 1974/5, he would pour himself a large gin and tonic and hide behind the sofa, ice trembling against the side of the glass.

Only then could he watch Lillee and Thomson batter

'There is no escape when you bat against the fastest bowlers. You can't fool yourself for long about your courage, or lack of it.'

War victims:
Mike Gatting,
Graham Gooch,
Steve Waugh …
Left: Maurice Leyland

It takes all sorts... Derek Randall (left) and Jack Russell

> '*All sorts of diverse human qualities may be enlisted in the fight: think of the eccentric antics of Derek Randall.*'

Greig and his teammates on helpful pitches. Courage is indeed one of the main qualities that we most admire in the figures we read about in this book.

So far I have spoken of the psychological qualities shown by the great battlers of sport, in cricket in particular. We all have experiences of moments of happiness when we feel freer than usual, on the go, with a sense of well-being and co-ordination. We all know even better how rarely this happens. I now want to say something about ways in which we lose touch with our confidence, courage, and capacity to respond with spontaneity allied to self-control. Needless to say, these failings,

everyday failings of us all, happen in all areas of life.

First, then, there are the problems of self-doubt. A judgmental inner voice tells us that we are no good. We focus on the weakest part of our armoury, losing touch with our real strengths. If we play well enough, we belittle our achievement by telling ourselves that the opposition are below par, or we have been lucky, or we would not have succeeded had there not been a cloudburst that distracted the other side. And so on.

We talk ourselves down, like parents whose children can never do well enough. And that may indeed be part of the origin of our shortcomings. Patronising parental voices, which we heard first along with our first attempts to crawl across the floor, may remain with us to the grave. We have come to identify with these childhood judges, and are liable, subtly or not so subtly, to treat our own children in similar ways. But such voices don't derive only from our

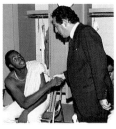

'On occasion, sporting struggles symbolise massive conflicts of history, which have informed life in ways that go far beyond sport.'

parents. We inhibit our own potency also from fear of our own unconscious emotions: we may be terrified both of our violent impulses, and of violent retaliation. Slow rivers run deep; quiet people may have unquiet currents that they themselves are unaware of.

We may, on the other hand, persistently over-rate, rather than under-rate, ourselves. We may become complacent, or arrogant, and lose concentration and focus. We may even alternate between grandiosity and timidity, swinging from one pole to the other. These swings are often the outcome of a constant subliminal processing, consisting of comparison and rivalry. We may without consciously realising it go around busily classifying others

either as second-rate or as immensely superior. We then become carelessly superior towards the first group, and intimidated and inhibited in the company of the latter. We are, in other words, hidden bullies.

I could go on. But this is not a psychological treatise. It is a book to be enjoyed, relished, read with tremors in the stomach, even from behind the sofa. For sport is a symbol for many aspects of life, and this is why it appeals to us so deeply. Maybe by reading the pages that follow we may imbibe a little of the daring, the poise under pressure, and the sheer guts shown by the protagonists in Cricket's Greatest Battles.

West Indian jubilation in Barbados after beating South Africa. Above: A meeting we thought we'd never see – Courtney Walsh of the West Indies with South African cricket supremo Dr Ali Bacher

When the force is with you

WAUGH V GIBBS · HEADINGLEY · 1999

SOUTH AFRICA V MALCOLM · THE OVAL · 1994

BOTHAM V AUSTRALIA · HEADINGLEY · 1981

Opposite: Steve Waugh lays waste to South Africa in their Super Sixes encounter in the 1999 World Cup

This page: Herschelle Gibbs, Devon Malcolm, Ian Botham

STEVE WAUGH
V
HERSCHELLE GIBBS

Steve Waugh

(New South Wales & Australia)
Aged 34. Australia's captain in both forms of the game since the stepping-down of Mark Taylor at the start of the year. Playing his 259th one-day international, with 5,928 runs to his credit at the start of the match.

Herschelle Gibbs

(Western Province & South Africa)
Aged 25. Playing his 31st one-day international. Had scored 210 in this World Cup, with a top score of 91 before this match. Renowned as a fielder almost in the Jonty Rhodes class.

STEVE WAUGH

HERSCHELLE GIBBS

The day Waugh broke out

World Cup group match · Headingley · June 13, 1999

The world saw Steve Waugh as a grafter rather than a dynamic one-day match-winner. But what did the world know? When his moment came in this do-or-die World Cup game, there was no way Steve Waugh was going to roll over and die. And in that pivotal moment, century-maker Herschelle Gibbs saw his own world turn to bitter ashes...

It may seem a little unfair to single out Herschelle Gibbs as Steve Waugh's antagonist in this battle, because in effect it was Waugh against the rest – a classic stand-off between the lone Aussie gunslinger and Sheriff Cronje's posse. But it was Gibbs's century that set up the confrontation; it was Gibbs's dropped catch that proved the turning point; and it was Waugh's defiance of the psychological pressure exerted by the rapacious South African fielders – led by Rhodes and Gibbs – that gave him his finest hour.

It had not been an unreservedly glorious World Cup for Australia so far. They had struggled to reach this 'Super

Six' stage, and defeat by South Africa would eliminate them from a tournament they had started as one of the favourites.

Their three victories in their group matches had been against Scotland, Bangladesh and the West Indies, none of whom had qualified for the Super Six – and under the rules of the tournament, only points gained against other qualifiers were carried over to the next stage. So Australia began that league stage with no points. They could not afford to drop any points now.

There had been signs that, since their earlier defeats by New Zealand and Pakistan, Australia had started firing on all cylinders again and certainly their first Super Six match

Herschelle's 'Gibbsy' bracelet failed to bring him luck when he came up against Steve Waugh at Headingley

Herschelle Gibbs on his way to a fine century which, sadly for him, was overshadowed by one calamitous moment in the field

at Chelmsford, thus eliminating England. But normal service had been resumed now and in the Super Six they had beaten Pakistan and New Zealand to qualify for the semi-finals. Pakistan and New Zealand were also through, while Zimbabwe would be keeping an anxious eye on Headingley. If South Africa could beat Australia, Zimbabwe would be in the World Cup semi-finals for the first time.

> *'You've just thrown away the World Cup.'*
> STEVE WAUGH TO HERSCHELLE GIBBS

At the heart of South Africa's innings, after they had won the toss, was a century from Herschelle Gibbs. He batted through to the 45th over, eventually bowled by McGrath for 101. His second-wicket stand with Cullinan, who made 50, had put on 95 in twenty overs, but it was Gibbs' departure that brought the real explosion, as tended to happen in this World Cup, with the advent of Lance Klusener. From 21 balls he clubbed 36, with a six and four fours. Jonty Rhodes had also contributed a lively 39 and the feeling was that South Africa's 271 for 7 would take some overhauling.

When both the Australian openers, Adam Gilchrist and Mark Waugh, had gone for five apiece and it was 20 for 2 in the sixth over, it seemed an even stiffer task, which became harder still with Steve Elworthy's second wicket – Damien Martyn for 11.

So, in the twelfth over, at 48 for 3, in came the captain, Steve Waugh. Already the required rate was pushing towards six an over, but there was an air of the Western desperado about Waugh, with little to say as he surveyed the enemy through narrowed eyes. There was steely calculation about his approach and no indecent haste. Australia's future in this competition depended on him and he was happy to accept the responsibility.

Waugh's partner was Ricky Ponting, a scamperer of a batsman. He hooked Elworthy for one huge six, but the pair saved the main assault for the fifth South African bowler, which amounted to ten overs shared by Hansie Cronje and the left-arm spinner Nicky Boje. The first fifteen overs had brought 54 runs, but the next fifteen produced 95 and took Waugh and Ponting past their hundred partnership. Klusener, already one of the heroes of the World Cup, returned to produce some magic and in

was a resounding win over India. Five days later they had a bit of a scare thanks to the batting of Neil Johnson before they overcame Zimbabwe at Lord's. But they still would need to beat the new tournament favourites, South Africa.

The South Africans had swept all before them in the group stage, until – astonishingly – they lost to Zimbabwe

Lance Klusener, above, told Waugh he was out when Gibbs 'caught' him – but the umpire begged to differ. Left: Mark Boucher sends the bails flying but Waugh scrambles home. The force was truly with the Aussie…

the 31st over it seemed that he had. At 152 for 3, Waugh played a short-arm pull at Klusener straight to Gibbs – a formidable fielder at midwicket.

Australian hearts sank. They knew that this was the decisive wicket. Gibbs, as his hands made contact with the ball, started to throw the ball up in celebration.

But the roar for the wicket changed to groans from South Africans as the ball was seen rolling away from the fielder. Some were mystified. Those Australians who had seen the end of their chances now laughed with relief.

Waugh admitted later to thinking that it might just possibly have been out, and Klusener arrived in his crease to tell him that it was.

But the umpire, Peter Willey, ruled in the face of South African queries that Gibbs had not been in control of it

before he dropped it. Waugh had been given a 'life' at 56.

Afterwards the story would be told that Waugh had informed Gibbs that he had thrown away the World Cup. Whatever the truth of that, the mortified Gibbs must have felt a growing certainty that his part in this match would be remembered more for this error than for his fine century.

Four overs later Klusener did break the partnership, as Ponting skied him to Donald at mid-on. He had made 69 and helped Waugh add 126 in 23 overs. Australia still needed 98 from fifteen overs, but now, joined by Michael Bevan – no stranger to Headingley – the magnificent Waugh was in full control and keeping Australia on course. They entered the last ten overs with six wickets in hand needing 66 more. In the 43rd over Waugh reached his hundred from 91 balls, having hit two sixes and ten fours.

Right: Eleven Aussies go mad at Edgbaston as Lance Klusener is run out and Australia go into the World Cup Final. Above: Tears of disbelief for a Springboks fan, while the kangaroos get sky-high at Headingley

Just before the last fearsome burst from Donald and Pollock, Bevan fell to Cronje for 27 but, difficult as those two great bowlers could make life, the determined Waugh was not going to let this one slip away now. With two balls to go in the final over, Australia were home and had kept themselves in the World Cup.

Steve Waugh was 120 not out and Ian Chappell can rarely have had an easier decision on the man of the match.

The result ought to have meant less to South Africa, who were in the semi-finals anyway. But they now found that their semi-final opponents were … Australia.

It really should have been the Final, but it provided the most astounding encounter of the tournament, when Allan Donald was run out in the last over to tie the match.

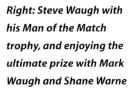

Right: Steve Waugh with his Man of the Match trophy, and enjoying the ultimate prize with Mark Waugh and Shane Warne

Australia v South Africa

Headingley, Leeds, England		13.6.1999
South Africa won the toss and batted		
Australia won by 5 wickets		

South Africa

G.Kirsten	c Ponting b Reiffel	21
H.H.Gibbs	b McGrath	101
D.J.Cullinan	b Warne	50
*W.J.Cronje	lbw b Warne	0
J.N.Rhodes	c Waugh b Fleming	39
L.Klusener	c Warne b Fleming	36
S.M.Pollock	b Fleming	3
+M.V.Boucher	not out	0
N.Boje		
S.Elworthy		
A.A.Donald		
Extras	b-0, lb-7, w-8, nb-6	21
TOTAL	(in 50.0 overs, for 7 wickets)	**271**

Fall of Wickets	1-45	2-140	3-141	4-219	5-250
	6-271	7-271			

Bowling Analysis	O	M	R	W
G.D.McGrath	10	0	49	1
D.W.Fleming	10	0	57	3
P.R.Reiffel	9	0	47	1
T.M.Moody	8	1	56	0
S.K.Warne	10	1	33	2
M.G.Bevan	3	0	22	0

Australia

M.E.Waugh	run out	5
+A.C.Gilchrist	b Elworthy	5
R.T.Ponting	c Donald b Klusener	69
D.R.Martyn	c Boje b Elworthy	11
*S.R.Waugh	not out	120
M.G.Bevan	c Cullinan b Cronje	27
T.M.Moody	not out	15
S.K.Warne		
P.R.Reiffel		
D.W.Fleming		
G.D.McGrath		
Extras	b-0, lb-6, w-7, nb-7	20
TOTAL	(in 49.4 overs, for 5 wickets)	**272**

Fall of Wickets	1-6	2-20	3-48	4-174	5-247

Bowling Analysis	O	M	R	W
S.M.Pollock	9.4	0	45	0
S Elworthy	10	1	46	2
A.A.Donald	10	0	43	0
L.Klusener	10	0	53	1
W.J.Cronje	7	0	50	1
N.Boje	3	0	29	0

Umpires: P.Willey, S.Venkataraghavan
Man of the Match: S.R.Waugh

Suddenly that Headingley result four days before became crucial, as it put Australia into the World Cup Final.

At Lord's on June 20 Australia annihilated Pakistan. Steve Waugh is a pragmatic character, if ever there was one, but as he raised the trophy, he must have felt the elation of knowing how his own remarkable effort had – almost singlehandedly – clawed his side back into the reckoning.

CRICKET'S GREATEST BATTLES

NASSER HUSSAIN'S ANALYSIS

'*Mentally he is the strongest player I've played against – he's the toughest*'

'*Most of it, Nass, is kidding the opposition.*'

STEVE WAUGH ON CRICKET'S MIND GAMES

This was a classic moment for Steve Waugh. Up to then he had been a very good but not great one-day player. Whenever England played him we viewed him as a bit of a nurdler; someone who would contribute, but not a Michael Bevan. However, Steve is a little bit arrogant – and he wants to be remembered as the best. If he was going in at 150 for 3 and could get a good 40, that would be nice. But when he walked out there at 48 for 3, a part of him would have said: "I've got a chance to do something special here."

Looking back, he wouldn't have it any other way, because in effect this was the innings that won the World Cup.

Shortly before the tournament, Australia had toured Pakistan and I think that Waugh had developed some new shots such as the slog sweep, which made him into a much better one-day player. He had started to hit the ball into unorthodox areas, which is what Bevan does. Steve Waugh is almost like the golfer Jim Furyk with his big loopy swing. He knows he's not an elegant front-foot player like his brother, but he knows his game – and he knows the mental side of batting better than anyone else.

Mentally he is the strongest player I've played against.

He's the toughest. I remember having a drink with him in a bar after we lost the 1998 Test in Adelaide. We were both a bit drunk – and that's the only time you can ask Steve Waugh anything about how great he is. So I did. His answer was: "Most of it, Nass, is kidding the opposition."

The way he sees it, some of the English batsmen walk in to bat looking a bit shy and it's obvious that McGrath and Warne have already got a hold over them. That's why Waugh always walks out with a big strut and swagger, with his little red handkerchief hanging out of his pocket, really looking like he wants to get out there.

He taps his wicket, takes his time, has a good look round. His body language says: "This is where I want to be" – even though he himself admits that, like everyone else, that first half hour is scaring the living daylights out of him. He is full of nervous energy but he'll never show that to the opposition.

So at 48 for 3 he had nothing to lose. I don't think the Australians sitting there in the balcony at Headingley were expecting him to win them the game. He admitted afterwards that he said to himself: "Right, I'm going to enjoy this," taking his mind off the seriousness of the situation.

NASSER HUSSAIN'S ANALYSIS

'When Waugh hit the ball to Gibbs and Gibbs dropped it, that was the key moment not just of the game, but of the whole tournament.'

'After you drop a catch, every boundary that bloke hits weighs on your mind...' Waugh gives Gibbs something else to think about

The game really swung when he hit the ball to Herschelle Gibbs and Gibbs dropped it. I know that Herschelle has been bombarded with it ever since, but that was the key moment not just of the game, but of the whole tournament. Waugh and Ponting had put on 110 together. In that sort of situation the fielding side are looking for any half-chance to get back into the game – and that would have been it.

Then, the longer Waugh's innings drags on after the dropped catch, the more Gibbs's teammates are going round thinking, "I wish he'd taken that catch." As captain, you're thinking: "If Gibbs had caught it, they would now need eight an over, not six an over."

Then in the next game, when they met again, as the situation got tighter and tighter, I'm sure the South Africans would all have been thinking: "We had the opportunity to end this four days ago and they're still here and they're still at us. Is their name on the Cup?"

It does play mind games with you. I've been there. There's nothing worse than dropping a catch, especially in an international. As a batsman, when you're out you've messed up your day. But you drop a catch and afterwards every boundary that bloke hits, every single run he gets, weighs on your mind. Every time he nicks it, you're hoping it will be caught – "Get me out of jail, put me out of my misery."

When Graham Thorpe dropped Matthew Elliott on the same ground in 1997, and Elliott went on to get 199, that

NASSER HUSSAIN'S ANALYSIS

A decisive moment at Headingley: Herschelle Gibbs is bowled by Glenn McGrath for 101. Below: Graham Thorpe was devastated after he dropped Matthew Elliott during his match-winning 199

absolutely killed Thorpe. It ruined his batting. Every evening driving home he would start off talking about the catch and how he saw it. I would try to change the subject because the more he dwells on it, the more it undermines him.

For Gibbs, it was even worse because he had already scored a hundred. That sums up the game of cricket: you've got a century, your side's coasting to victory, what a great feeling, we're beating Australia, the old enemy, the side South Africa can never beat in any sport at all. And all of a sudden you drop a catch and that bloke's taken them to victory and you've got to play them again in the semi-final. It just shows that one moment in cricket can completely ruin your day and, in this case, completely ruin the tournament.

I remember, when I was a young player at Essex, I took a

diving slip catch and as I got up I casually tossed the ball away. Graham Gooch came up and told me in no uncertain terms: "Don't do that – make sure the umpire gives them out first." Only Herschelle will know whether he dropped that catch due to showmanship, but it certainly looked like it.

Up to that moment, everything Gibbs had done in the field was sheer elegance. You have him and Jonty Rhodes on either side of the wicket and that casual arrogance is part of their double act, the way they catch it and throw it up dismissively as if to send you off with disdain.

When you're batting, it intimidates you. But in this situation his greatest asset proved very costly.

It's said that Waugh told Gibbs he had thrown away the World Cup. That certainly sounds like Steve Waugh. He does play it tough. He is a master at saying things that get into your head. When he chirps you from gully, he says all the things you don't want to hear. A lot of the Aussie chirps are aimless insults, but he'll try to play on your mind in a way that affects your performance.

Waugh knew that was a very, very important moment. In the next game, the South Africans would remember that they had had the chance to put them away – and you have to take those chances, especially when you're playing Australia. When you play, with all respect, England, you get four or five moments in a day; when you play Australia you get one. *Carpe diem* – seize the day.

An incident like that has an effect on the whole team. You find the weaker ones mentally will mention it more and more. They'll forget that Gibbs got 100, or that they personally bowled badly or whatever. They'll focus on the dropped catch. I don't know the South African side, so I don't want to pass comment, but I can imagine the response of sides that I have captained. At midnight in the bar, after you've lost, the strong people in your side will be saying: "Maybe I should have got a few more runs," but others will be sitting in the corner saying: "If he'd taken that catch, that would have been it, game over."

It does put a few bad vibes through the outfit – and of course it was Sod's Law that the next game there they were again in a close situation. That's where the mind games come into play – and you never know, it could explain what happened in the last over of the semi-final, when Lance Klusener and Allan Donald were involved in that suicidal run-out. Klusener

had batted brilliantly all through the tournament and whatever happened in that last over was just in the mind.

That little passage from when Waugh came in strutting his stuff, with nothing to lose, to the moment when Gibbs dropped the catch – that was when Australia won the World Cup.

'Steve Waugh is a master at saying things that get into your head. When he chirps you from gully, he'll try to play on your mind in a way that affects your performance.'

Left: Who holds the balance of power now? Steve Waugh and opposing captain Hansie Cronje after the Super Six match

SOUTH AFRICA
V
DEVON MALCOLM

SOUTH AFRICA'S JONTY RHODES

DEVON MALCOLM

'You guys are history'

Third Test • The Oval • August 20, 1994

*It's the most famous one-liner in cricket, a riposte worthy of Clint Eastwood in Unforgiven.
The South African fielders thought they could laugh at Devon Malcolm with impunity.
Two fistfuls of wickets later, England's gentle giant of a fast bowler showed them
how it felt to be truly unforgiven*

Devon Malcolm's battle, in 1994, was perhaps more with the chairman of the England selectors, Ray Illingworth, than with South Africa. After an injury in the West Indies at the start of the year, Malcolm had returned to the England side for the First Test against New Zealand at Trent Bridge. The paceman took two wickets as England overwhelmed the opposition. He was in the squad of 13 summoned to Lord's for the Second Test but didn't play, and was not selected for the Third Test as England registered another draw to win the series 1-0.

The main event of the season, though, was going to be the arrival of the South Africans for their first Test series in

WHEN THE FORCE IS WITH YOU

THE PROTAGONISTS

South Africa
Recently returned to world cricket, but already making a mark, led by Kepler Wessels, who had had a successful Test career with Australia before becoming the first captain of the new South Africa.

Devon Malcolm
(Derbyshire and England)
Aged 31. Born in Jamaica, but playing his 28th Test for England. The fastest bowler in England's attack, started this Test with 101 wickets to his credit.

Devon Malcolm rehearses his speech after being hit on the helmet by Fanie DeVilliers

England for 29 years. Lord's provided the scene for the historic return and the visitors rose to the occasion with a crushing 356-run win, though their limelight was rather stolen by the 'dirt in the pocket' affair involving the England captain, Mike Atherton. The Second Test was drawn at Headingley. And so to the final Test at The Oval...

Despite not having played for England since June, Devon Malcolm still felt he had a chance of being recalled. He took the precaution of setting off for Derbyshire's game at Hove over the weekend of the team announcement with his England kit packed in the car. His faith was rewarded.

The following Thursday he was sharing the new ball

Devon Malcolm during his nine-wicket spell. A first-innings bouncer had felled Jonty Rhodes and forced him to spend the night in hospital

with Phil DeFreitas in a four-pronged seam attack. The second wicket fell to Malcolm – Peter Kirsten bowled by a leg-stump yorker.

But more significant was the incident three overs after lunch, when Jonty Rhodes ducked into one of Malcolm's bouncers, denting the little South African's helmet and causing him to be taken off to an overnight stay in hospital.

Rhodes did not return in the innings, but by the end of that first day South Africa had recovered from a wobbly 136 for 5 to a happier 326 for 8.

They added only six runs next day, but England made a poor start in reply, and half an hour before the close they had slumped to 222 for 7. But in that last half-hour, Darren Gough and Phil DeFreitas ignited popular support with a rollicking stand for the eighth wicket. Fifty-nine runs came in eight overs, and 11 more the next morning

before DeFreitas and then Joey Benjamin fell, bringing in Malcolm in his accustomed place at number 11.

Having sent Rhodes to hospital, he was greeted by a barrage of comments from the close fielders, principally advising the bowler, Fanie DeVilliers, to return the compliment. And he did. Malcolm did not see the ball that clattered into his helmet grille.

It was not so much the blow as the continued remarks from the South Africans, calling for more of the same, that got under his skin, as he recovered. He turned to the slips and said: "You guys are dead. You guys are history."

South Africa did not pay any great price to Malcolm the batsman. He holed out for four and England were all out for 304, 28 runs behind. But 45 minutes into that Saturday morning, Devon Malcolm had a new ball in his hand.

He had been encouraged by his teammates in his still-burning fury, which was about to rebound on South Africa's batsmen. After a maiden over from DeFreitas, Malcolm sent his first ball whistling past Gary Kirsten's nose. Two balls later the ball ballooned off Kirsten's bat handle into Malcolm's hands as he followed through. South Africa were no runs for one wicket.

In his next over, Gary's half-brother Peter Kirsten

South African captain Kepler Wessels, above, and his successor Hansie Cronje were probably Malcolm's most notable victims

hooked a bouncer to deep fine leg, where DeFreitas took the catch. 1 for 2. There had been time for the batsmen to cross while the ball was in the air, bringing Hansie Cronje on strike, and in the same over Malcolm got one to nip back in and take his middle stump. 1 for 3.

This was heady stuff for a large Saturday crowd.

Kepler Wessels, the captain, was joined by Daryl Cullinan, and either side of lunch they added 72 together for the fourth wicket. But half an hour after lunch Malcolm was back, bowling round the wicket to the left-handed Wessels, who edged a drive to Steve Rhodes behind the stumps. 73 for 4.

With Rhodes still not ready to bat, Brian McMillan had moved up to number six, but he had been at the heart of

South Africa's first-innings revival with an innings of 93 and now with Cullinan added 54 for the fifth wicket. Again it was Malcolm who ended the stand, as McMillan edged another lifting ball to Thorpe in the slips. South Africa were 137 for 5.

Tea was taken at 143 for five and Malcolm had the ball in his hand for the first over after the interval. Dave Richardson found himself squared up to a late-swinging ball and trapped LBW. 143 for 6.

In the same over, Craig Matthews got a glove to a rapid delivery which Steve Rhodes leapt to catch. It was 143 for 7, as Jonty Rhodes now reappeared, and Devon Malcolm had taken all seven.

At the former home ground of Jim Laker, people were

'A sizeable bump was coming up on my head, but after a couple of tablets, a glass of water and a lump of ice on the spot, I was ready to roll...'

DEVON MALCOLM, 'YOU GUYS ARE HISTORY!'

England v South Africa

The Oval, London, England
South Africa won the toss and batted

18.8.1994 - 21.8.1994
England won by 8 wickets

South Africa	1st innings		2nd innings	
G.Kirsten	c Rhodes b DeFreitas	2	(2) c & b Malcolm	0
P.N.Kirsten	b Malcolm	16	(1) c DeFreitas b Malcolm	1
W.J.Cronje	lbw b Benjamin	38	b Malcolm	0
*K.C.Wessels	lbw b Benjamin	45	c Rhodes b Malcolm	28
D.J.Cullinan	c Rhodes b DeFreitas	7	c Thorpe b Gough	94
J.N.Rhodes	retired-injured	8	(9) c Rhodes b Malcolm	10
B.M.McMillan	c Hick b DeFreitas	93	(6) c Thorpe b Malcolm	25
+D.J.Richardson	c Rhodes b Benjamin	58	(7) lbw b Malcolm	3
C.R.Matthews	c Hick b Benjamin	0	(8) c Rhodes b Malcolm	0
P.S.de Villiers	c Stewart b DeFreitas	14	not out	0
A.A.Donald	not out	14	b Malcolm	0
Extras	(b-8, lb-10, w-1, nb-18)	37	(b-0, lb-5, w-0, nb-9)	14
TOTAL	(for 9 wickets declared)	332	(all out)	175

Fall of Wickets	1-2	2-43	3-73	4-85	5-136	1-0	2-1	3-1	4-73	5-137
	6-260	7-266	8-301	9-332		6-143	7-143	8-175	9-175	10-175

Bowling Analysis	O	M	R	W	O	M	R	W
P.A.J.DeFreitas	26.2	5	93	4	12	3	25	0
D.E.Malcolm	25	5	81	1	16.3	2	57	9
D.Gough	19	1	85	0	9	1	39	1
J.E.Benjamin	17	2	42	4	11	1	38	0
G.A.Hick	5	1	13	0	2	0	11	0

England	1st innings		2nd innings	
G.A.Gooch	c Richardson b Donald	8	b Matthews	33
*M.A.Atherton	lbw b de Villiers	0	c Richardson b Donald	63
G.A.Hick	b Donald	39	not out	81
G.P.Thorpe	b Matthews	79	not out	15
A.J.Stewart	b de Villiers	62		
J.P.Crawley	c Richardson b Donald	5		
+S.J.Rhodes	lbw b de Villiers	11		
P.A.J.DeFreitas	run out	37		
D.Gough	not out	42		
J.E.Benjamin	lbw b de Villiers	0		
D.E.Malcolm	c subs b Matthews	4		
Extras	(b-1, lb-0, w-1, nb-15)	17	(b-0, lb-6, w-0, nb-7)	13
TOTAL	(all out)	304	(for 2 wickets)	205

Fall of Wickets	1-1	2-33	3-93	4-145	5-165	1-56	2-180
	6-219	7-222	8-292	9-293	10-304		

Bowling Analysis	O	M	R	W	O	M	R	W
A.A.Donald	17	2	76	3	12	1	96	1
P.S.de Villiers	19	3	62	4	12	0	66	0
C.R.Matthews	21	4	82	2	11.3	4	37	1
B.M.McMillan	12	1	67	0				
W.J.Cronje	8	3	16	0				

Umpires: R.S.Dunne, K.E.Palmer   **Man of the Match:** D.E.Malcolm

Prime Minister John Major congratulates a British winner

starting to contemplate the prospect of another England bowler taking all ten in an innings. Such speculation was ended after an eighth-wicket stand of 32, when Gough had Cullinan caught at slip for 94. It was an important enough wicket for Malcolm to forgive the Yorkshireman for spoiling his party. It was 175 for 8.

At the same score, Rhodes showed an uncharacteristic, if understandable, reluctance to move his feet into the line of a ball from Malcolm and was caught behind. 175 for 9.

Donald, the last man, was bowled off his pads, to give Malcolm his ninth wicket. South Africa were all out for 175 and Malcolm had taken nine for 57 in sixteen-and-a-half overs. Malcolm, having registered the sixth-best figures in all Test cricket, was mobbed by his disbelieving teammates and given a standing ovation by a jubilant Oval crowd.

England still had what might be an awkward 204 to win, with an hour to go on the third day. They lost Graham Gooch that evening, but when Atherton was the second man out for 63, the job was almost done. By one o'clock the playing area was covered with picnickers celebrating England's series-levelling eight-wicket victory, while Devon was uncorking the Champagne and chatting with Prime Minister John Major on the Lord's balcony.

Devon Malcolm – who was once famously misnamed as Malcolm Devon by Ray Illingworth's predecessor, Ted Dexter – became overnight one of the best-known cricketers in England. His battle with South Africa had been decisively won. His battle with Ray Illingworth was to continue.

NASSER HUSSAIN'S ANALYSIS

'Devon had been hit on the head – that helped him!'

To put in a really good performance, any cricketer needs three or four things going for him, and in this match Devon Malcolm had that and more. First, there was his conflict with Ray Illingworth, the chairman of selectors. They had never gelled as long as they had been working together. Illy had criticised him in public, and Malcolm had been left out since the beginning of the summer, so he would have used that to spur him on.

Then there's the crowd at The Oval. When you're doing well, they really get behind you and it's a great atmosphere. So that was another thing in Devon's favour.

The third thing he had going for him was the pitch at The Oval, which was then the quickest wicket in England.

The previous year, when we beat Australia there, Dev bowled really quickly and took six wickets.

He is a very fast bowler. His assets are sheer pace and intimidation. He is also awkward to bat against, because he bowls quite wide on the crease, leans wide of the sightscreen with his arms and legs going in all directions, and makes it hard for you to see the ball coming.

Dev's problem was there was always a conflict between how he wanted to bowl and how England wanted him to bowl. They wanted him to become a classical bowler who could swing it away, which I don't think he was ever going to be. I would have tried to refine him a little bit without taking away his natural asset – which was to run up and hurl it as fast as he can. On

'If you take the mickey out of his batting in the nets, don't bat next because he'll be steaming in.'

Left: Devon gets hit – let battle commence!

NASSER HUSSAIN'S ANALYSIS

'Devon really is a lovely quiet bloke. But if you have a dig at him, just be careful.'

certain wickets, such as Barbados or Perth, Devon Malcolm would be a real handful, as he proved that day at The Oval.

The fourth thing in Devon's favour was that he had been hit on the head – that helped him!

And finally there was his batting…

Now one thing you have to realise about Dev is that he absolutely loves his batting. He takes his nets very seriously and if you take the mickey out of his batting, don't bat next because he'll be steaming in. After he was hit on the head, he got a few chirps from the South African fielders – and

Dev would have seen that as someone taking the mickey out of his batting, and he doesn't like that.

There are some people you should chirp and some you shouldn't, and Dev is one of those. He really is a gentle giant. I've been on many a tour with him, I've been out with him and his family, he has driven me out to see things in Jamaica and he's a lovely quiet bloke. But if you have a dig at him, just be careful.

On the 1990 visit to the West Indies I was partnered with Alec Stewart for the tour show and Alec had the idea of

sending Devon up. In those days Malcolm used to wear thick glasses and he was having serious catching problems. Mickey Stewart, the coach, used to shout: "Right hand, Dev!", to make him concentrate on catching with his right hand. So in the show I put on four pairs of glasses, Alec would throw the ball to me shouting "Right hand, Dev!", and I would drop it and fall over a table.

Everyone was laughing, but I don't know how funny Dev found it, apart from the fact that the next day in the Barbados nets everything was aimed at my throat.

However, generally speaking Devon is the exception to the rule. I've played in some teams that take the view that you shouldn't sledge the opposition fast bowler, but I don't agree. If you are playing the likes of Ambrose and Walsh, there's no point going round being matey with them, because you're going to get bouncers anyway. No matter how many drinks Atherton has with Donald after the game, it won't stop him bowling a bumper first up the next morning.

Glenn McGrath is a bowler you do want to wind up, because he doesn't bowl so well when he's annoyed. So

NASSER HUSSAIN'S ANALYSIS

'If you are playing the likes of Ambrose and Walsh, there's no point going round being matey with them, because you're going to get bouncers anyway.'

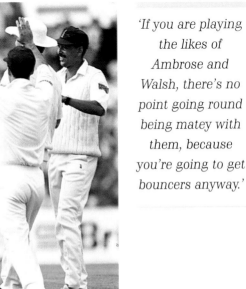

Malcolm mobbed by his teammates – a sight which became ever more familiar as the innings went on

when he comes in to bat, if he has had a chirp at me, which he often has, and he's backing nervously away to the legside, as he often does, I'll say: "Come on, Glenn, get behind it son," and give him a bit of stick.

But you do have to make sure you chirp the right bloke. In my young days at Essex, whenever Monte Lynch of Surrey came in to bat, Keith Fletcher used to say: "Just keep quiet, lads. If you wake him up, you're in trouble." Because when Monte was stirred up, he could tear you apart.

Sometimes it's better not to annoy your opponent – and that's what South Africa discovered to their cost about Devon Malcolm when they unwisely had a go at him at The Oval.

IAN BOTHAM
V
AUSTRALIA

IAN BOTHAM

AUSTRALIA'S KIM HUGHES

The resurrection of Botham

Third Test · Headingley · July 16-21, 1981

*If ever a match showed the importance of psychology in cricket, this was it.
The Australians stood on the brink of a crushing victory. But when England's players
managed to pick themselves up off the canvas, the momentum of the battle
changed in a way that still seems utterly incredible*

Headingley '81 has become a watchword for hope in impossible cricketing situations. Even those who witnessed it can – years afterwards – scarcely believe what they saw. As much as anything else, it was the start of a remarkable turnaround in the fortunes that year of one man – Ian Botham. 'Beefy' had been appointed England captain at the start of the previous year, when Mike Brearley had told the selectors that he did not want to tour any more. It had not been a happy experience, though he was unfortunate that nine of his first ten Tests in charge were against the formidably powerful West Indies.

By the end of the Second Ashes Test of 1981, his

WHEN THE FORCE IS WITH YOU

THE PROTAGONISTS

Ian Botham
(Somerset & England)
Aged 25. Playing his 38th Test, he started the match with 1,612 runs and 174 wickets. In this series he was to make 399 runs with two centuries and take 34 wickets. His final 5,200 runs and England record 383 wickets makes him one of the great all-rounders of history.

Australia
Despite the return of the Packer players in 1979, Kim Hughes's team were not considered favourites to recapture the Ashes until their win in the First Test. The bowling – Lillee, Lawson, Alderman and Bright – was more impressive than the batting.

Where's that one gone? Botham's unpredictability set Australia an insoluble problem

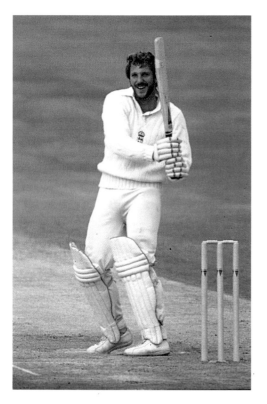

Guy the Gorilla's finest hour – nonchalantly hooking Geoff Lawson for four, bowling his way to a six-wicket haul in the first innings, and driving Terry Alderman to distraction

captaincy record was Played 12, Won 0, Lost 4, Drawn 8. Botham resigned, pleading the need to be appointed for more than one Test at a time. His form with the bat had suffered, having only passed fifty in the first of the 21 innings he had played as captain, from which he had made 276 runs at an average of only 13. His bowling had held up better, with a haul of 35 wickets, but the pair of noughts in the Lord's Test against Australia seemed to mark the point at which he had to relinquish his captaincy – though he was always eager to deny that it had affected his form.

With England 1-0 down after two Tests, the selectors turned back to Brearley, under whom England had enjoyed success during the period when the cricket world had been hit by the Packer revolution. He called Botham to see if he had the will to play in the next Test at Headingley. Botham reassured him of his keenness. Brearley was delighted. "I think you'll get 150 runs and take ten wickets," he declared.

On a cold, cloudy morning, England opted for four seamers, with only Peter Willey to provide spin. Kim Hughes took his time to decide to bat after winning the

toss for Australia, and by the close of the first day at 203 for 3, it seemed like a good decision. Botham had taken the first wicket, but John Dyson had gone on to make 102. The next day Australia crawled to 400, with Botham taking five more wickets to finish with six for 95. At 401 for 9 they declared in order to have a crack at the England openers before the close, but Boycott and Gooch survived.

The Saturday was another bleak day and even bleaker for the England batting. The pitch was producing enough unpredictable bounce to make that Australian score look very useful and, in Lillee, Alderman and Lawson, Australia had a fine seam attack to exploit it.

Half the side were out with only 87 on the board when Botham came in, determined that no one was going to dictate the terms to him. Playing with a freedom that belied the situation, he rattled up fifty from only 54 balls, but then gloved a sharply lifting ball from Dennis Lillee to wicketkeeper Rod Marsh.

His appearance had lifted the gloom for a while, but not long after his departure England were all out for 174 –

227 behind. Kim Hughes asked them to follow on. Thanks to bad light, there was not much of that third day left, but enough for Lillee to have Gooch caught at slip and England in a sorry state at 6 for 1 when the umpires stopped play. There could be no doubt of the outcome. Barring a monsoon, Australia must surely win after the rest day, either on Monday or Tuesday.

Infamously, Ladbrokes offered odds of 500 to 1 against an England victory. It aroused comment – and, it was revealed much later, the financial interest of two members of the Australian team, Messrs Lillee and Marsh – but no one truly thought that those were unrealistic odds. Certainly the two teams, who gathered on that Saturday night for a barbecue at Ian Botham's house, can have had no doubt of the outcome.

On Monday morning many hotel bills were settled in expectation of a fourth-day finish. That predicted state of affairs was only reinforced as England slumped to 41 for 4 – the wickets shared by Lillee and Terry Alderman. Resistance at last came as Peter Willey joined Geoff Boycott. They put on 64 together, but it was only delaying the inevitable and when Lillee removed Willey for 33 half an hour after lunch, in came Botham at 105 for 5. England were still 122 runs behind.

There was nothing to start with that suggested remarkable events in the offing. Over the next ten overs Botham took most of the strike. A boundary off Alderman and a couple more off Lillee had taken him to 22 when Boycott was LBW to Alderman for 46. Bob Taylor came in, but he fell victim to Alderman's next over for one.

At 135 for 7, England still needed 92 just to make Australia bat again. In the home team's dressing room, kit-bags were being packed and Mike Brearley was beginning to rehearse the losing captain's version of events for the inevitable press conference.

Botham was 23 and Graham Dilley was the new man in. Three boundaries through the covers off Alderman and Lawson in his first five overs at the crease took the Kent fast bowler to 23 and seemed to light the spark in Botham. After tea he started to launch into the normally miserly

> *'I think you'll get 150 runs and take ten wickets.'*
> MIKE BREARLEY
> TO IAN BOTHAM ON THE EVE OF THE MATCH

Alderman, who had resumed the bowling after the interval, continuing a spell which was already ten overs old. Botham brought up his second fifty of the match – made from 57 balls – with a four over the slips' heads; the first of four boundaries in one over. Dilley, meanwhile, was taking plenty of runs off Lillee, no less. England, 51 runs behind at tea, took only 43 balls afterwards to avert the innings defeat. Two overs later Dilley reached a fine half-century, with his eighth boundary, cracking Lillee through the off side.

Dilley fell at last, bowled by Alderman coming round the wicket for 56. In eighty glorious minutes, he and Botham had added 117 for the eighth wicket, entertained the crowd and irritated the Australians, who had believed they were on the brink of victory.

But at 252 for 8, just 25 ahead, the fun was almost certainly over. The new batsman was Chris Old, joining Botham now in full flow against the three Australian fast bowlers, as Hughes persisted with the form of attack that had initially got them into this strong position. Old, too, rose to the occasion, with some fine strokes of his own and saw Botham to a remarkable century as he swung his 87th ball, bowled by Lawson, away to the boundary for four more. His second fifty had come in a mere 30 balls.

The lead was beginning to become more relevant by the time Geoff Lawson bowled Old for 29. It was 319 for 9 and that ninth-wicket stand had taken England 92 runs ahead. They had ensured a fifth day's play for the Test and that in itself was quite an achievement. After all, while there was life there was hope and it might rain.

Even Bob Willis, coming in at number 11, was doing his bit with his celebrated forward defensive lunge. Botham was now manipulating the strike so that in the twenty minutes to the close Willis had only to face five balls, from which he made one run, while his partner ensured that England added another 32 to give them a lead of 124. And still there was life. England were 351 for 9 and the amazing Botham 145 not out.

There was much re-booking of hotels to be done and much speculation, too. Surely this had only been a glorious

Graham Dilley, Ian Botham's batting accomplice, scored a fine 56

Above: John Dyson was Australia's top scorer with 102 in his first innings.
Right: Bob Willis on his way to figures of eight for 43, and Ian Botham, hero of the hour

'The truth is that it was just one of those crazy, glorious one-off flukes. To be perfectly honest, when I went out to bat I wasn't really interested in the state of the match at all.'

IAN BOTHAM
IN 'BOTHAM –
MY
AUTOBIOGRAPHY'

piece of defiance in the face of inevitable defeat. "Well," said some wise old heads, "a bit more resistance in the morning could take the lead past 150. This isn't a great pitch. You never know what might happen!"

In the event England managed only another five – surely not enough – before Willis gave Alderman his sixth wicket of the innings. The whole country, though, was raving about Ian Botham and his 149 not out.

It had been fun, but Australia now had most of the day to score only 130 to win.

On a hunch, Brearley opened the attack with Botham, hoping that the adrenalin was still pumping. It paid off in the third over, when Australia had reached 13, with the wicket of Wood, caught behind for 10. After two unaffordably expensive overs from Dilley, Willis came on, bowling up the hill, but the score mounted past fifty.

Brearley at last moved his quickest bowler to the top end and Bob Willis began the greatest spell of his career.

He started it with the wicket of Trevor Chappell, caught behind off a bouncer. Then he struck a double blow on the stroke of lunch. Hughes was snapped up by the charmed Botham, low at third slip, and Graham Yallop caught at short leg off a rearing lifter. Three wickets had fallen for the addition of two runs and now it was 58 for 4 as they went in to lunch.

For the first time people were allowing themselves to believe that an extraordinary victory for England might be a possibility. All around the country radios were tuned to

the events in Leeds, as the players took the field after lunch.

Australia had gathered seven more precious runs when Chris Old, coming up the hill, bowled Allan Border, leg stump, for the third duck of the innings. In the next over Dyson fell to Willis, caught behind, hooking. It was 68 for 6 and the specialist batting had gone.

Rod Marsh was no mean obstacle, though. So in Willis's next over England were delighted to see him hook an enormous skier that Dilley caught right on the fine leg boundary. It was 74 for 7 and in his next over it was 75 for 8, when Lawson was caught behind for one.

Suddenly, almost incredibly, the odds favoured England.

But there were still not over-many runs to play with. England's supporters had to grit their teeth through the apparent extravagance of several no-balls from Willis and through an agonising eighth-wicket stand, when it seemed that England's hopes had been raised only to be dashed.

Lillee and Ray Bright put on 35, before Mike Gatting dived forward at mid-on to take a low catch off Lillee for 17 and give Willis his seventh wicket.

Australia were only 20 runs away from their target, but now they had just one wicket in hand.

In Willis's next over it was ended with Bright yorked for 19. Australia had been bowled out for 111. England had won by 18 runs and had become only the second team in Test history to win a match after following on. Bob Willis had taken eight for 43 – but the heroics of Botham the previous day had been the reason that he had had the chance to bowl at all.

England had squared the series. They were to go on to win two scarcely less remarkable Tests at Edgbaston and Old Trafford, to make sure of retaining the Ashes.

You probably don't need reminding that the hero of both matches would again be the incredible Ian Botham.

England v Australia

Headingley, Leeds, England
Australia won the toss and batted

16.7.1981 - 21.7.1981
England won by 18 runs

Australia

	1st innings		2nd innings	
J.Dyson	b Dilley	102	c Taylor b Willis	34
G.M.Wood	lbw b Botham	34	c Taylor b Botham	10
T.M.Chappell	c Taylor b Willey	27	c Taylor b Willis	8
*K.J.Hughes	c & b Botham	89	c Botham b Willis	0
R.J.Bright	b Dilley	7	(8) b Willis	19
G.N.Yallop	c Taylor b Botham	58	(5) c Gatting b Willis	0
A.R.Border	lbw b Botham	8	(6) b Old	0
+R.W.Marsh	b Botham	28	(7) c Dilley b Willis	4
G.F.Lawson	c Taylor b Botham	13	c Taylor b Willis	1
D.K.Lillee	not out	3	c Gatting b Willis	17
T.M.Alderman	not out	0	not out	0
Extras	(b-4, lb-13, w-3, nb-12)	32	(b-0, lb-3, w-1, nb-14)	18
TOTAL	(for 9 wickets declared)	401	(all out)	111

Fall of Wickets	1-55	2-149	3-196	4-220	5-332	1-13	2-56	3-58	4-58	5-65
	6-354	7-357	8-396	9-401		6-68	7-74	8-75	9-110	10-111

Bowling Analysis

	O	M	R	W	O	M	R	W
R.G.D.Willis	30	8	72	0	15.1	3	43	8
C.M.Old	43	14	91	0	9	1	21	1
G.R.Dilley	27	4	78	2	2	0	11	0
I.T.Botham	39.2	11	95	6	7	3	14	1
P.Willey	13	2	31	1	3	1	4	0
G.Boycott	3	2	2	0				

England

	1st innings		2nd innings	
G.A.Gooch	lbw b Alderman	2	c Alderman b Lillee	0
G.Boycott	b Lawson	12	lbw b Alderman	46
*J.M.Brearley	c Marsh b Alderman	10	c Alderman b Lillee	14
D.I.Gower	c Marsh b Lawson	24	c Border b Alderman	9
M.W.Gatting	lbw b Lillee	15	lbw b Alderman	1
P.Willey	b Lawson	8	c Dyson b Lillee	33
I.T.Botham	c Marsh b Lillee	50	not out	149
+R.W.Taylor	c Marsh b Lillee	5	c Bright b Alderman	1
G.R.Dilley	c & b Lillee	13	b Alderman	56
C.M.Old	c Border b Alderman	0	b Lawson	29
R.G.D.Willis	not out	1	c Border b Alderman	2
Extras	(b-6, lb-11, w-6, nb-11)	34	(b-5, lb-3, w-3, nb-5)	16
TOTAL	(all out)	174	(all out)	356

Fall of Wickets	1-12	2-40	3-42	4-84	5-87	1-0	2-18	3-37	4-41	5-105
	6-112	7-148	8-166	9-167	10-174	6-133	7-135	8-252	9-319	10-356

Bowling Analysis

	O	M	R	W	O	M	R	W
D.K.Lillee	18.5	7	49	4	25	6	94	3
T.M.Alderman	19	4	59	3	35.3	6	135	6
G.F.Lawson	13	3	32	3	23	4	96	1
R.J.Bright	4	0	15	0				

Umpires: D.G.L.Evans, B.J.Meyer   **Man of the Match:** I.T.Botham

NASSER HUSSAIN'S ANALYSIS

'Botham had nothing to lose – and that was exactly the situation he needed'

'The Australians would have been getting more and more frustrated, not just at the score mounting up but also at the bizarre way the runs were being scored.'

In some ways, the battle here was Ian Botham against himself. In the space of two days he went from an all-time low to an all-time high. He had suffered a complete loss of form, however much he claims he hadn't. He had just lost the captaincy. Everyone was slagging him off. Then he found himself in a situation where he had nothing to lose – and that was exactly what he needed.

This was the classic example of a guy hitting his way back into form. When you are out of form, there are too many bees buzzing in your head: you notice everything and you can't focus. You can't get in the zone because you're worried about your form. I had been out of nick in 1998 when we needed to set a quick target in Barbados, and I saw it as a good chance to play my shots. I began playing much more freely, and after that I went on to get runs in Antigua.

David Gower probably played like that all the time, but I remember him saying to me that when he was out of nick he would go in, even in a Test, and try to hit every ball for four. A get-them-before-they-get-me mentality. As Keith Fletcher says, it's only a couple of boundaries from being out

of form to being in form. You can have a net where you just don't know where your bat is and your feet aren't moving – and then you go in to bat, you get a couple of loose balls, hit a couple of good shots and that's it, you're off and running.

Even the greatest players sometimes need to re-establish their self-belief. Graham Gooch, for instance, could get very down when he was out of form. He would say silly things like, "I can't bat, I've lost it" – and this was a bloke who had scored 120 first-class hundreds. The same goes for Botham, even if he might not say it out loud. However outwardly big and confident he appears, he's like anyone else. But you could see during that innings against Australia that it was all starting to come right again.

Graham Dilley's role was important, not least because if he had got out quickly then the game had gone. It was important that the two of them were enjoying themselves and having a laugh. Meanwhile, the Australians would have been getting more and more frustrated, not just at the score mounting up but also at the bizarre way the runs were being scored. You don't mind so much if someone hits you

Alderman in metronomic action: 'Perfect for Beefy to attack'

follow on and they need 227 to make you bat again, the closer they get to it, the more angry you become. Every run hurts you. There's nothing worse for an opener than having to go in and knock off 10, because he personally has nothing to gain. He either nicks one and gets out – and that's really going to ruin his celebration – or he's going to be six not out and no one remembers that.

Option A: If we bowl them out for 220 I go up to the dressing room and open a bottle of Champagne and we get drunk and I don't even have to unpack my gear.

Option B: If they get 240 I've got to go up there, get my mind right, get all my gear out and put it on and sit there and focus and go through all my mind games.

There's a big difference there.

A lot of cricket is about momentum. If you can get the last three or four men out quickly, the momentum of the whole side when they go off to prepare to bat is on an up. Whereas if you're not getting that last couple of wickets and your openers are out on the field wondering when they're going to bat and your bowlers are a bit down because their figures have been ruined, then the momentum of the game has been changed slightly – especially in a game like that where Australia were supposed to have won it already.

Then the fact that it went into the fifth day helped England, because it delayed it for the Australians. They'd have been expecting it to be all over on the fourth day. Now there's a fifth day and the momentum has shifted even more. There's a whole evening and night of thinking, "Hey, we can't actually lose this game, can we?" You've been all over them for three-and-a-half days and suddenly Botham's a hero and the press are saying England can win. I can imagine a whole evening of it really building up the pressure on them.

So when they finally got England out on the last morning and went back into the dressing room, Kim Hughes had a trickier problem than Mike Brearley.

If you are chasing a small total, the captain has to tell his players: "Don't leave it to anyone else." When your team's at 56 for 1 and cruising, you don't want the batsmen in the middle thinking: "We've won the Test, where are we going tonight? I'll hit a few shots and show I can play a little bit." And you don't want the guys in the dressing room sitting there thinking: "Fifty for 1, I'm not going to get in." The key

through the covers for four, but when the guy is flaying it over the slips it hurts much more.

It was interesting that Alderman was the first bowler they got after. If you let him bowl at you, he loves it because, like Angus Fraser, he's a metronomic bowler who likes to be in control. But because he is so predictable, they knew where he was going to bowl so he was perfect for Beefy to attack.

Also, consider the effect this partnership was having on the Australian batters. If you have made the opposition

NASSER HUSSAIN'S ANALYSIS

'Switching Willis to Botham's end was a classic bit of decisive captaincy, because if it's not happening when the opposition are chasing a small total, you have to keep changing things around. You just need one thing to happen...'

Mike Brearley, author of a historic victory, and Bob Willis, who delivered the punchline

thing if you are 50 for 1 is to try to make it 130 for 1. Don't think, "Oh, we can win it on 130 for 5, it doesn't matter, a win's a win." After five hard days of a Test match, the toughest bit is to finish it off because people are mentally tired. You mustn't think, "Might as well pack my bag while the other boys are knocking these runs off" – that's a dangerous mind-set to get into. And it's no good thinking, "I'll get 20 and we'll knock them off between us." Generally you need a good 70 not out from someone to be sure.

So in the Australian dressing room, Kim Hughes had his work cut out. Over in the England dressing room, you couldn't have had a better combination than Brearley and Botham. You can imagine Beefy, after all he had been through, having scored 149 not out to put his team 124 ahead – he would have been as pumped up as anything. He would have been going around bashing people on the arm, saying: "Come on, we can win this."

Mike Brearley would have been a great foil for that. Inside, he was probably just as excited, but he needed to be a calming influence. The worst thing you can do as captain in a situation like that is to say: "Come on, boys, we can win this," because that puts the pressure on your team and some of them will start thinking, "Are we favourites now?"

I would have just said: "Come on, boys, you never know… Maybe someone can make a name for themselves here." I can imagine Brearley doing that.

He gave Botham the new ball. That was probably the obvious thing to do. But then to switch Willis to Botham's end, that was a classic bit of decisive captaincy, because if it's not happening when the opposition are chasing a small total, you have to keep changing things around. You just need one thing to happen – and Willis coming steaming in down the hill was probably it.

It must still give Kim Hughes nightmares.

NASSER HUSSAIN'S ANALYSIS

'In the England
dressing room,
you couldn't have
had a better
combination than
Mike Brearley and
Ian Botham.'

*Ian Botham enjoys a
well-earned cigar after
his glorious innings*

In the line of fire

BRADMAN V LARWOOD · AUSTRALIA · 1932/3

GREIG V LILLEE · BRISBANE · 1974/5

RANDALL V LILLEE · MELBOURNE · 1977

CLOSE V HALL · LORD'S · 1963

Opposite: Derek Randall falls to that oh-so-familar combination ... c Marsh b Lillee
This page: Battered batsmen Don Bradman, Bob Willis (felled by Lillee at Brisbane in 1974), Derek Randall, Brian Close

DON BRADMAN
V
HAROLD LARWOOD

Don Bradman

(New South Wales & Australia)
Aged 24. His 18 Tests before this series had brought him 2,695 runs and he was to finish in 1948 having made 6,996 runs from 52 Tests at the amazing average of 99.94.

Harold Larwood

(Nottinghamshire & England)
Had his 28th birthday on the tour. He had played 16 Tests before the tour and would not play another after it. In this series he would take 33 of his eventual 78 wickets.

DON BRADMAN

HAROLD LARWOOD

The 100 years war begins
England tour to Australia • 1932 - 33

The Bodyline Affair was not just a quarrel between two sports teams.
Without Bodyline, there would have been no Lillee and Thomson, no Holding or Ambrose,
Trueman or Donald. Intimidation in cricket began in 1932. It sparked a diplomatic incident
– and the aftershocks are still being felt today

Don Bradman played his first Test in 1928 against an England team that reads like a Who's Who of cricketing greats and which beat Australia by the huge margin of 675 runs. The Englishman who took six first-innings wickets was the small fast bowler from Nottinghamshire – Harold Larwood. He went on to take 18 wickets in the series, but not that of Bradman, who made 478 runs from the four Tests he played in.

Larwood finally managed to claim Bradman's wicket in his last innings of the 1930 series in England. At The Oval he had him given out caught behind (a somewhat questionable decision) … but not until Bradman had made

232. He had scored 974 runs in the series and Larwood had suffered at least as much as any other England bowler. Clearly Bradman was going to be a thorn in England's flesh when they returned to Australia in two years' time.

However, in that innings at The Oval, there were a few around the England camp who thought they had seen some pointers to the way to curb the prodigious scoring of this remarkable run-machine. As plans for the 1932 series were being laid, Larwood was asked if he thought he could be accurate enough to bowl 'leg theory' – aiming at the leg stump, with a packed leg-side field to dry up the flow of runs. In his habitual matter-of-fact way, almost surprised that anyone needed to ask him, he agreed that he probably could. "We'll have to wait and see about that," he said.

Once in Australia, in a match before the Tests against 'An Australian XI', the England vice-captain, Bob Wyatt, standing in for Douglas Jardine, for the first time took 'leg theory' up a stage as Larwood bowled very fast and short to that restrictive field. 'Bodyline' was born – and, significantly, Bradman fell cheaply in each innings to Larwood.

Leg theory in action: Six England fielders ring the leg side as a ball from Harold Larwood flies past the Australian captain Bill Woodfull

Jack Fingleton and Don Bradman go out to bat at Melbourne – the only match Australia won, even though Bradman was bowled for a duck

Woodfull, Bradman and Bertie Oldfield, who was also hit by Larwood

Bradman had been in a tangle with the Australian Cricket Board over a contract with a newspaper, which had even threatened to jeopardise his playing in the series, but it was illness that kept him out of the First Test in Sydney, which England won – without 'bodyline' tactics – by ten wickets.

Bradman returned for the Second Test in Melbourne, cheered to the echo when he came out to bat in the first innings, only to be bowled first ball by Bill Bowes. This was the Test in which Jardine first really instructed his fast bowlers to bowl 'bodyline'. But on a slow pitch, with England having made the mistake of leaving out their spinners, Bradman made an undefeated hundred in the second innings and Australian disgust at English tactics was submerged in a series-levelling victory.

In mid-January the Third Test was begun in Adelaide. England recovered from a poor start to make 341. The Saturday afternoon crowd was abuzz as the Australian batsmen came out to face the England fast bowlers. 'Gubby' Allen, an amateur, who was able to tell Jardine that he refused to bowl 'bodyline', was taking the new ball with Larwood and rewarded his captain with the wicket of Fingleton for nought in his first over. Larwood also did not bowl 'bodyline' while the ball was new. However, at the end of his second over he made a ball rear from not much short of a length and it struck the Australian captain, Bill Woodfull, a fearful blow over the heart.

For the start of Larwood's next over to Woodfull, Jardine, never one to shy away from a chance of antagonising the crowd – and conscious, probably, of trying to rattle the new batsman at the non-striker's end – called up the array of short legs that constituted the 'bodyline' field.

That new batsman was Bradman and, though Woodfull weathered the storm, it was Bradman who fended a lifting ball from Larwood into the leg trap to be out for 8.

Later in that innings Bertie Oldfield, the Australian wicketkeeper, was also hit by Larwood, though again not in his 'bodyline' mode. It all fuelled crowd unrest and sparked a hastily-drafted telegram from the Australian

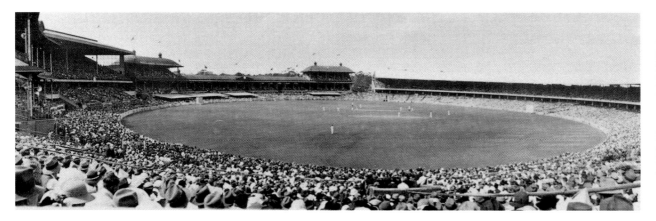

A 68,000 crowd saw Australia win at the MCG. Below: A woman models the body armour worn by some of the Australian batsmen (she wasn't actually a member of the team). Known as the 'anti-leg-trap guard', it was designed by the Australian captain, Bill Woodfull. Really!

Cricket Board to the MCC protesting at the tactics and calling them 'unsportsmanlike'.

England took a first-innings lead of 119 and batted Australia out of the match with a second innings of 412. Bradman made 66 in the second innings and it was Hedley Verity who claimed his wicket, though Larwood finished with four – seven in the match, which England won by 338 runs.

There was much diplomatic activity in the three weeks up to the Fourth Test in Brisbane. The MCC grandees, back home in London, hadn't actually seen bodyline in action, and couldn't believe that an England captain would employ the tactics of which the Australians accused Jardine. So when they received a telegram saying he was unsportsmanlike, of course they bristled.

There was noticeably less crowd anticipation in Brisbane than there had been in Adelaide. Before the Third Test, the man in the Australian street had believed that his hero, Don Bradman, had the answer to 'bodyline'. Now he was not so sure. In fact Larwood failed to take a wicket on the first day, as Bradman reached 71. But early on the second day, indulging his usual way of scoring against Larwood's leg theory of trying to make enough room to force him through the off side, he lost his leg stump for 76.

The match is most famous for the heroics of Eddie

Paynter, rising from his hospital bed to make 83 and gain England a slender first-innings lead. That was followed by some ferociously fast bowling by Larwood at Bradman, which appeared to lead Woodfull into trying to take more of the bowling. Eventually it was the same tactic of trying to use the space on the off side that accounted for Bradman, when he cut Larwood to a lonely cover fielder for 22. Larwood's only other wickets in that innings came from the tail but, as far as his captain was concerned, he had done his job in getting Bradman. England won the match by six wickets and with it regained the Ashes.

Years later, Bradman ruefully explained how he had been undone by Jardine's tactics: "They had five men close in on the leg side; maybe two or even three behind square. And two men out on the boundary; one just behind square leg and another finer. Now, with the ball being pitched short and rising round about chest or head high, if you play a defensive shot, it's very difficult indeed to keep it out of the hands of one of these short leg fieldsmen. If you play the hook shot, it's very difficult to avoid hitting it down the throat of one of those two fellows out on the fence, so there's really nowhere to go.

"With seven men on the leg side, the only place you can score runs with any certainty at all is on the off side.

Jardine, Larwood and Gubby Allen, who said no to bowling bodyline

'He is a queer fellow. When he sees a cricket ground with an Australian on it, he goes mad.'

SIR PELHAM WARNER ON JARDINE, 1934

Gubby Allen's snaps– top, from left: Governor of Queensland with England's Nawab of Pataudi and Pelham Warner. Centre: Jardine and Herbert Sutcliffe launch 'First Test'. Bottom: Les Ames, Hedley Verity, J W Pike and Eddie Paynter on a boat from Brisbane to Sydney

And this is very difficult to do when the ball is coming straight at your body and it's round about chest high.

"The easiest way not to be hit when you're playing a fast bowler who's bowling the ball short is to move inside the line and let it go down the leg side. So what I did put me in much greater danger of being hit than if I had adopted an

'Bodyline bowling has assumed such proportions as to menace the best interests of the game, making protection of the body by the batsmen the main consideration. This is causing intensely bitter feeling between the players as well as injury. In our opinion it is unsportsmanlike. Unless stopped at once, it is likely to upset the friendly relationships existing between Australia and England.'

TEXT OF THE CABLE FROM THE AUSTRALIAN CRICKET BOARD TO THE MCC FOLLOWING THE ADELAIDE TEST, 1933

orthodox method, but there was no way that I was going to get runs playing orthodox cricket and I hoped that by doing that I might force them to change their field. But over the whole series I was not successful enough to force them to change their field. And I'm sure no one ever could do this against a man of Larwood's pace and accuracy."

The Don was hit by Larwood for the first time in the series at Sydney in the final Test – although only on the upper arm – but he was again bowled leg stump by him when he had made 48. Famously, after taking four for 98, Larwood was sent in as nightwatchman and on the third day took his score to 98. In the second innings Larwood, after inflicting a 'pair' on Vic Richardson, subjected Bradman and Woodfull to the usual barrage, but this time the risky batting tactics seemed to work.

Larwood's series was about to end painfully, as he broke his foot bowling. He was, quite naturally, keen to go off. "No you don't, Harold," said Jardine and made him finish the over before putting him at mid-off, just where Bradman could see him and might believe that he would return. So it was Verity who dismissed Bradman for the last time in the series. "Now you can go, Harold," said Jardine and

Australia v England

The Ashes Test Series	Australia 1932/33	

| **1st Test** – Sydney | 2.12.1932 - 7.12.1932 | |
England won by 10 wickets		
Australia 1st innings	360 all out	
S.J.McCabe 187 not out	H.Larwood 5-96	
England 1st innings	524 all out	
H.Sutcliffe 194	T.W.Wall 3-104	
W.R.Hammond 112		
Nawab of Pataudi 102		
Australia 2nd innings	164 all out	
J.H.W.Fingleton 40	H.Larwood 5-28	
England 2nd innings	1-0	

| **2nd Test** – Melbourne | 30.12.1932 - 3.1.1933 | |
Australia won by 111 runs		
Australia 1st innings	228 all out	
J.H.W.Fingleton 83	W.Voce 3-54	
D.G.Bradman 0	H.Larwood 2-52	
England 1st innings	169 all out	
H.Sutcliffe 52	W.J.O'Reilly 5-63	
Australia 2nd innings	191 all out	
D.G.Bradman 103 not out	W.R.Hammond 3-21	
	H.Larwood 2-52	
England 2nd innings	139 all out	
H.Sutcliffe 33	W.J.O'Reilly 5-66	

| **3rd Test** – Adelaide | 13.1.1933 - 19.1.1933 | |
England won by 338 runs		
England 1st innings	341 all out	
M.Leyland 83	T.W.Wall 5-72	
R.E.S.Wyatt 78		
E.Paynter 77		
Australia 1st innings	222 all out	
W.H.Ponsford 85	G.O.B.Allen 4-71	
D.G.Bradman 8	H.Larwood 3-55	
England 2nd innings	412 all out	
W.R.Hammond 85	W.J.O'Reilly 4-79	
L.E.G.Ames 69		
D.R.Jardine 56		
Australia 2nd innings	193 all out	
W.M.Woodfull 73 not out	G.O.B.Allen 4-50	
D.G.Bradman 66	H.Larwood 4-71	

| **4th Test** – Brisbane | 10.2.1933 - 16.2.1933 | |
England won by 6 wickets		
Australia 1st innings	340 all out	
V.Y.Richardson 83	H.Larwood 4-101	
D.G.Bradman 76		
W.M.Woodfull 67		
England 1st innings	356 all out	
H.Sutcliffe 86	W.J.O'Reilly 4-120	
E.Paynter 83		
Australia 2nd innings	175 all out	
L.S.Darling 39	G.O.B.Allen 3-44	
D.G.Bradman 24	H.Larwood 3-49	
England 2nd innings	162-4	
M.Leyland 86	H.Ironmonger 2-47	

| **5th Test** – Sydney | 23.2.1933 - 28.2.1933 | |
England won by 8 wickets		
Australia 1st innings	435 all out	
L.S.Darling 85	H.Larwood 4-98	
S.J.McCabe 73		
L.P.J.O'Brien 61		
W.A.S.Oldfield 52		
D.G.Bradman 48		
England 1st innings	454 all out	
W.R.Hammond 101	P.K.Lee 4-111	
H.Larwood 98		
H.Sutcliffe 56		
R.E.S.Wyatt 51		
Australia 2nd innings	182 all out	
D.G.Bradman 71	H.Verity 5-33	
M.W.Woodfull 67	H.Larwood 1-44	
England 2nd innings	168-2	
W.R.Hammond 75 n.o.	H.Ironmonger 2-34	
R.E.S.Wyatt 61 not out		

Right: Leo O'Brien is skittled by Larwood.

Above left: England's Eddie Paynter hits out

> '*We, Marylebone Cricket Club, deplore your cable. We deprecate your opinion that there has been unsportsmanlike play. We have fullest confidence in captain, team and managers and are convinced they would do nothing to infringe either the Laws of Cricket or the game.*'
>
> PART OF MCC'S CABLED REPLY, 1933

the two prime protagonists walked off the ground together.

England won that match by eight wickets and the series 4-1. Harold Larwood had taken 33 wickets, including Bradman four times, but he was never selected by his country again and was even diplomatically prevented from playing against the Australians for Nottinghamshire on their next visit to England in 1934.

Don Bradman had made 396 runs at an average of over 56. By his amazing standards, he regarded that as failure.

NASSER HUSSAIN'S ANALYSIS

'Jardine simply used the laws to the fullest extent'

Cricket was a more gentlemanly game in those days, so I can see why Bodyline caused a few ructions. However, I'm with Jardine on this one. He may not have been the greatest of players, but to my mind he was a great captain.

Trying to come up with new ideas is surely what the game's about. These days it always seems to be the foreign cricketers who produce something different, like the Pakistanis suddenly reverse-swinging it at 100mph. Why can't we in England make these break-throughs? So I think Jardine should be held in high esteem for trying to do something new.

As a captain, you're always looking for another angle – especially if you're up against someone like Bradman. If you can negate a key player's performance, you have to try it. Jardine had looked at the laws and found a way to use them

Woodfull's nemesis: Douglas Jardine, captain of the MCC, on the deck of the Orient liner Orontes, bound for Australia

to the fullest extent. It's no different to asking a spinner to keep landing it in the rough outside leg stump. This was more body-threatening, but I'm sure it was done purely for tactical reasons, rather than being malicious.

Of course, there is the question of whether it was within the spirit of the game, which the captain is always being reminded of. But to a modern player, this was. If you did it now, no one would bat an eyelid because we get hit all the time. I got hit by Allan Donald in South Africa and was amazed to find that two months later I still had the bruises. In today's game you get hit on the head then turn round and watch it in slow motion on the giant screen.

Of course, in those days they didn't have helmets, and people were quite seriously hurt. But even so, Bodyline was ingenious. It's not often that someone devises a completely new approach to field positionings. To even think about setting such a radical leg-side field, let alone do it, required a really inventive mind.

In the pictures from that era, it's noticeable that a lot of the players had strong bottom hands and so would tend to hit everything 'over to my side'. Even with Jim Laker, the off-spinner, you see people being caught round the corner. In a later era, when you watch film of Keith Fletcher and MJK Smith, you see a lot of leg flicks, perhaps because they played on uncovered wickets

'He (Jardine) can be a powerful friend but a relentless enemy. He gives no quarter and asks none. He is a fighter, every inch of him. He will see a job through, no matter what the consequences, and will never admit defeat.'

– 'BODYLINE' TOUR BOWLER
BILL BOWES, 1949

and the ball bounced and stopped a little bit. So you can see how the leg theory field came about.

There are only three ways to play short-pitched bowling aimed at your ribs. Either you get out of the way and you don't get any runs; or you hook; or you fend. And in the 1930s, when you could have as many fielders behind the wicket on the leg side as you wanted, whether the batsman hooked or fended, the percentages were against him.

So with this particular tactic, there was no get-out

NASSER HUSSAIN'S ANALYSIS

'If you did it now, no one would bat an eyelid because batsmen get hit all the time.'

Modern-day warfare, as Dominic Cork gets one between the eyes. Left: Douglas Jardine at the crease

clause: whatever the batsman did, he was doomed.

Now that only two fielders are allowed behind the wicket on the leg side, the fielding team can cover one of the options, but not both. So someone like Steve Waugh will fend it off whereas I will have a hook. If you've got one of the

**Larwood with fellow
Notts and England
paceman Bill Voce
(centre) at the Ashes
celebration dinner at the
Dorchester in July 1933**

*'Jardine's approach
obviously came as
a shock because
people were't used
to England being
ruthless and
playing it tough.
That's the
Aussie way...'*

two skills then you've solved the problem – and that's what cricket is all about, solving the problems.

Even with today's fielding restrictions, if the bowler tries to hit the batsman on the head or in the ribs, you can set a field that makes it very hard to play. If you have two men out on the hook and men in close on the leg side, and the bowler uses the width of the crease to angle the ball in, or comes round the wicket like Allan Donald did to Atherton and me at Trent Bridge in 1998, it's difficult to combat it.

Mark Waugh counters it in the way Don Bradman did, by standing out to the leg side and trying to hit over the slips. When Waugh first did that to the West Indies, they accused him of being scared. But he wasn't. That's just his way of countering a Bodyline-style attack. I remember him lifting Donald into the stand over third man at Essex. If you had

never seen him before it would have looked like a tail-ender backing away in fear, but it was a regulation shot.

These days, a Bodyline attack is normal cricket. The only difference is that you can't have seven fielders on the leg side. The instigator of what you might call the new Bodyline era was Clive Lloyd – and he too used the laws of the game to their fullest extent. In Lloyd's day, they didn't have the rules we have now about over-rates, so it didn't matter how slowly the West Indies bowled their overs, and he was able to keep four very aggressive fast bowlers going all day.

It's all very well to have a plan, but you still need players who can carry it out. Jardine's plan required very accurate fast bowlers and that's what he had in Larwood and Voce.

I think all of these things add to the game. Recently in India, Anil Kumble was opening the bowling in a Test. That's

Jack Fingleton of Australia ducks a bouncer from Larwood during the Second Test at Melbourne

an equally radical departure from the norm. Even when India do open with a fast bowler, he's often just a sandpaper bowler, the aim being to take the shine off the ball as quickly as possible for the four spinners.

All these different challenges are an important part of the game. That's why it's called Test cricket. It is a test, and if it was easy anyone could do it. In 1932, Australia would have picked their best players and if they weren't up to facing that type of bowling, that's hard luck.

I can see why the law about legside fielders was changed after Bodyline. But even if the laws hadn't been changed, people would have found the way to combat it – for instance, by wetting the wicket so that it became lifeless.

> *'With this tactic, there was no get-out clause: whatever the batsman did, he was doomed.'*

And in the end, the great players like Don Bradman would have worked out how to play Bodyline bowling. That's why the Tendulkars and the Waughs are great players, because if they had any kind of weakness against any type of bowling, in any country and any conditions, they wouldn't be averaging 55 – or, in Bradman's case, 99.

Jardine's approach obviously came as a shock because people weren't used to England being ruthless and playing it tough. That's the Aussie way. So this was a welcome reversal of roles to nullify the local hero, Don Bradman. The Australians still go on about Bodyline, which is ironic considering the way they used Lillee and Thomson. But I suppose that's the whingeing Aussies for you.

TONY GREIG
V
DENNIS LILLEE

Tony Greig

(Sussex & England)
Aged 28. Born in South
Africa, playing his 34th
Test for England, having
made 2,044 runs.
Was to take over the
captaincy the following
year and lose it in 1977
over his involvement
with Packer.

Dennis Lillee

*(Western Australia
& Australia)*
Aged 25. Playing his
12th Test, having taken
51 wickets, 39 of them
in 7 Tests against
England. Returning
after missing a season
with a back injury.

TONY GREIG

DENNIS LILLEE

Tweaking the dragon's tail

First Test • Brisbane • November 30 & December 1, 1974

*When England began firing head-high balls at Dennis Lillee and Jeff Thomson,
they didn't know what they were letting themselves in for. The response was fast and furious,
and by the time Tony Greig came in, half his teammates were out or in hospital.
So he came up with a cunning plan … to make Lillee even madder*

*Opposite: The biter bit.
England thought they
had the more dangerous
attack, but in the First
Test it was Bob Willis
who was felled by Lillee*

It was a confident MCC touring team that Mike Denness led to Australia at the end of 1974. That confidence was built substantially on the premise that Australia were short of genuine fast bowling. Eighteen months before, Dennis Lillee had returned from the West Indies with chronic back trouble and worries, too, about the fitness of his knee. With the strength of these two crucial parts of a fast bowler's body in doubt, no one in the England camp expected the man who had looked so dangerous in England in 1972 to be a serious threat.

Bob Massie, whose swing bowling had devastated England at Lord's in that 1972 series, had lost his control

'Just remember that they started it.'

DENNIS LILLEE, BEFORE HIS ONSLAUGHT

and his place and England saw no reason to worry about the calling-up for the First Test of a rather wild young fast bowler from Sydney called Jeff Thomson.

England, for this Brisbane Test, to be played on a pitch hastily prepared after storms by the Lord Mayor, Clem Jones, had two genuine fast bowlers, Bob Willis and Peter Lever, backed up by the remorselessly accurate fast medium of Mike Hendrick. That attack was in action on the first morning, when Ian Chappell had won the toss for Australia, and the two fast men quickly demonstrated that they would not be shy of using the

Australia v England

BCG, Brisbane, Australia
Australia won the toss and batted

29.11.1974 - 4.12.1974
Australia won by 166 runs

Australia	1st innings		2nd innings	
I.R.Redpath	b Willis	5	b Willis	25
W.J.Edwards	c Amiss b Hendrick	4	c Knott b Willis	5
*I.M.Chappell	c Greig b Willis	90	c Fletcher b Underwood	11
G.S.Chappell	c Fletcher b Underwood	58	b Underwood	71
R.Edwards	c Knott b Underwood	32	c Knott b Willis	53
K.D.Walters	c Lever b Willis	3	not out	62
+R.W.Marsh	c Denness b Hendrick	14	not out	46
T.J.Jenner	c Lever b Willis	12		
D.K.Lillee	c Knott b Greig	15		
M.H.N.Walker	not out	41		
J.R.Thomson	run out	23		
Extras	(b-0, lb-4, w-0, nb-8)	12	(b-1, lb-7, w-1, nb-6)	15
TOTAL	(all out)	**309**	(for 5 wickets declared)	**288**

Fall of Wickets 1-7 2-10 3-110 4-197 5-202
6-205 7-228 8-229 9-257 10-309

1-15, 2-39, 3-59, 4-173, 5-190

Bowling Analysis	O	M	R	W	O	M	R	W
R.G.D.Willis	21.5	3	56	4	15	3	45	3
P.Lever	16	1	53	0	18	4	58	0
M.Hendrick	19	3	64	2	13	2	47	0
A.W.Greig	16	2	70	1	13	2	60	0
D.L.Underwood	20	6	54	2	26	6	63	2

England	1st innings		2nd innings	
D.L.Amiss	c Jenner b Thomson	7	c Walters b Thomson	25
B.W.Luckhurst	c Marsh b Thomson	1	c Chappell b Lillee	3
J.H.Edrich	c Chappell b Thomson	48	b Thomson	6
*M.H.Denness	lbw b Walker	6	c Walters b Thomson	27
K.W.R.Fletcher	b Lillee	17	c Chappell b Jenner	19
A.W.Greig	c Marsh b Lillee	110	b Thomson	2
+A.P.E.Knott	c Jenner b Walker	12	b Thomson	19
P.Lever	c Chappell b Walker	4	c Redpath b Lillee	14
D.L.Underwood	c Redpath b Walters	25	c Walker b Jenner	30
R.G.D.Willis	not out	13	not out	3
M.Hendrick	c Redpath b Walker	4	b Thomson	0
Extras	(b-5, lb-2, w-3, nb-8)	18	(b-8, lb-3, w-2, nb-5)	18
TOTAL	(all out)	**265**	(all out)	**166**

Fall of Wickets 1-9 2-10 3-33 4-57 5-130
6-162 7-168 8-226 9-248 10-265

1-18 2-40 3-44 4-92 5-94
6-94 7-115 8-162 9-163 10-166

Bowling Analysis	O	M	R	W	O	M	R	W
D.K.Lillee	23	6	73	2	12	2	25	2
J.R.Thomson	21	5	59	3	17.5	3	46	6
M.H.N.Walker	24.5	2	73	4	9	4	32	0
K.D.Walters	6	1	18	1	2	2	0	0
T.J.Jenner	6	1	24	0	16	5	45	2

Umpires: R.C.Bailhache, T.F.Brooks

bouncer. Tony Greig, the tall, fair-haired, South African-born all-rounder, also liked his cricket to be confrontational and used his height to bang in his fair share of short balls.

In the final session of the first day, as Australia slid to a less than encouraging 205 for 6, Greig accounted for Lillee, with another bumper, caught behind. Fuming at the lack of respect shown by bouncing Australia's spearhead, Lillee arrived in the dressing room.

"Just remember that they started it," he declared to his teammates. "I'll bloody finish it, but they started it."

Next day, Australia managed to get to 309 before Lillee was able to start on carrying out his threat. But first it was the surprise package, Thomson, despite bowling into the breeze, who showed how dangerous he could be with steepling lift from not far short off a length. It accounted for both openers with only ten on the board and broke the thumb of Dennis Amiss. Lillee had John Edrich dropped on one, but bowled Fletcher after Max Walker had removed Denness.

That brought in Tony Greig, at 57 for 4, to join the already battered Edrich. Greig relished such a situation. "I

Left: G'day, sport... A fan congratulates Tony Greig on his century.

Opposite: Thomson's riposte... Greig is yorked in the second innings

just took up a position," he says, "that the best thing to do to Lillee in particular was to try to antagonise him, to make him bowl differently to the way he should have bowled. And, as a result of having a go at him, he tried to kill me."

As he launched his counter-attack, Greig carved Lillee over the heads of the slip fielders to the boundary, drove him through the covers – and signalled the fours himself, to the fury of the fast bowler. The Australian captain, Ian Chappell, admits that Lillee was probably expending too much energy in trying to knock Greig's head off.

Being Greig's batting partner, while this policy of enraging the fast bowlers was being applied, was a nerve-racking existence, but the England team found Lillee, Thomson and the rest visiting their dressing room at the close of play, armed with cold beers.

By then Greig had reached 40 and England were looking more healthy at 114 for 4. Early on the third morning, though, Lillee broke Edrich's right hand and Thomson had him caught at slip in the next over, after he had made 48 and added 73 with Greig for the fifth wicket.

But Greig just carried on his attacking policy, as Walker dismissed Knott and Lever cheaply.

Derek Underwood helped add 58 for the eighth wicket. It saw Greig to his hundred, the only one he made against Australia and the one he remembers best of his eight in Test cricket, "because it was in conditions that were really tough".

It was Lillee who eventually got his man, caught behind by Rodney Marsh, to square the duel. Greig's 110 had taken five hours and included 15 fours. It had kept England's first-innings deficit, which had seemed likely to be far greater, to 44 – though in the end six second-innings wickets for Thomson, including yorking Greig for 2, gave Australia victory by 166 runs.

Lillee was to gain Greig's wicket twice more in the series and, when he limped off the field in the Sixth and final Test at Melbourne, with Thomson already injured, the batsmen who had suffered so much cashed in. Greig himself made 89 and Edrich 70, while two other prime targets for the fast bowlers, Denness and Fletcher, made 188 and 146 respectively. England won that Test by an innings, but lost the series 4-1.

> *'I took a position that the best thing to do to Lillee was to antagonise him, to make him bowl differently. And, as a result of having a go at him, he tried to kill me.'*
>
> TONY GREIG

NASSER HUSSAIN'S ANALYSIS

'I'm not sure that I would have tried to wind up Dennis Lillee in Brisbane...'

'I don't think England had seen anything like it.'

Tony Greig was an unconventional bowler and, at times, an extraordinary batsman. Opposite: Lillee and Thommo go out Pom-hunting

This was the start of a new era for fast bowling, especially in Australia, with its history of varied attacks, and I don't think England had seen anything like it. The combination of Lillee and Thomson was lethal – Lillee with his classical outswing and bristling, in-your-face aggression, and Thomson the big blond slinger with a catapult action that made it hard to see where the ball was coming from. Rather like Devon Malcolm, he just tried to hurl it and hit the batsman on the foot or on the head. And, in those days before helmets, if he hit you, it hurt.

I remember on my first Caribbean tour sitting in the bar of the upside-down Hilton in Trinidad listening to

Gordon Greenidge and Jeff Dujon talking about the West Indies' 1975 tour to Australia. They were used to facing Holding and Roberts, but that was the first time they'd thought about wearing helmets. This was serious pace.

There have been quick bowlers in every era, but in my opinion cricket became a different game at that time. Every international team now has a genuine quick bowler, and it all dates back to the mid-1970s.

I'm not sure that I would have tried to wind up Dennis Lillee in Brisbane – and I can't imagine any batsman now signalling four after hitting a quick bowler to the boundary. But, having said that, trying to upset the bowler is a legitimate tactic – particularly when

Greig is one of those tall, in-your-face sort of people, and it obviously worked on this occasion. Keith Fletcher always speaks very highly of him. In this innings, Greig got 110 in about five hours, which is the normal pace for a Test match hundred, so it wasn't all just swashbuckling. But it was obviously very brave, not to say foolhardy, to deliberately provoke Lillee and Thomson when he didn't have a helmet.

Largely because of that series, Keith Fletcher is now viewed as someone who played spin bowling well but not the quicks. Yet I would have challenged anyone to go on that tour and smack it around the park.

I see that Fletch got 146 in the last Test, when Lillee and Thomson were injured. It shows how much better they were than anyone else: they made the difference, and changed the face of Australian cricket. That's the value of a match-

NASSER HUSSAIN'S ANALYSIS

'There have been quick bowlers in every era, but in my opinion cricket became a different game at that time.'

winner. Over the last 20 years, England were at their best when they had Ian Botham or Graham Gooch in their prime, because those guys could turn a game singlehandedly. However much you work on team spirit, you can't beat class.

Going back to Keith Fletcher, I was amused to hear recently that he managed to antagonise Lillee on the very first day of the 1975/76 series. Peter Lever bowled Lillee a bouncer and a voice came from the slips saying: "Give him another one." Lillee turned round with a glare and said: "Who said that?" Next day, when Fletcher came in to bat, Lillee went to the boundary to meet him and walked in with him. I don't imagine that he was just asking after his health…

he has a classical action like Lillee's. The only time I faced him, he was bowling little dobbers for Northamptonshire. But I think I would have been quite happy to get involved in a bouncer battle with Lillee when he was at his peak if it meant that he stopped pitching it up and swinging it, because that was when he was most dangerous.

DEREK RANDALL
V
DENNIS LILLEE

Derek Randall
*(Nottinghamshire
& England)*
Aged 26. Playing in his
fifth Test, at the end of
the tour in which he
made his debut.
Had made 86 runs in
his four Tests in India.
Also renowned as a
brilliant cover fielder.

Dennis Lillee
*(Western Australia
& Australia)*
Aged 27. Playing his
32nd Test, having taken
160 wickets already,
85 of them in his 17
Tests against England.

DEREK RANDALL

DENNIS LILLEE

The madcap laughs

Centenary Test • Melbourne • March 16 & 17, 1977

The way Derek Randall used to fidget at the crease as a paceman came pounding towards him, he often looked like a rabbit trapped in the headlights. When Dennis Lillee first saw him, he probably licked his lips at the thought of another easy English scalp. But then the batsman started raising his cap to Lillee's quickest bouncers, and the story got curiouser and curiouser

It was cricket's greatest party, held to celebrate 100 years of Test cricket and held on the same spot where Australia had beaten England by 45 runs exactly a century before. As befits such a great occasion, it was graced by the presence of Her Majesty the Queen, along with a host of the players from the pages of cricket history. The ghosts of many others were visibly and poignantly present in the pavilion, in the shape of the old name boards from the giant scoreboard which now lined the corridor walls.

England's team arrived in Australia in buoyant mood from their tour of India. Tony Greig had led them to victory there by winning the first three Tests. Their previous visit to

Not the usual gesture that a batsman makes to a fast bowler who has just tried to knock his block off... Derek Randall and Dennis Lillee exchange pleasantries during the Centenary Test

Australia had been two years before – the traumatic battering at the hands of Lillee and Thomson. Jeff Thomson had dislocated his collarbone at the start of the season and missed the rest of it, but Dennis Lillee was still a formidable presence in this side and three of England's batsmen went into the match with all too vivid memories of that tour.

Greg Chappell had taken over the Australian captaincy from his elder brother, Ian. He had shared the short home series against Pakistan, but beaten New Zealand in Auckland a few days before this match. He and Greig were escorted out to toss by all of the former England and Australia captains who were present, in front of a crowd in excess of 60,000. Reversing history, England won the toss. Greig invited Australia to bat and enjoyed an excellent first day.

First it was John Lever and Bob Willis who caused the mayhem, Willis even bowling Rick McCosker off his jaw, which sent the batsman straight to the X-ray room and confirmation of a fracture. At lunch Australia were 57 for 5. Only a stand of 51 for the sixth wicket between Greg Chappell and Rod Marsh gave any substance to the

innings, which was finished off by three wickets each for Chris Old and Derek Underwood. With England replying to Australia's 138 that evening, Lillee removed Bob Woolmer cheaply, but nonetheless the visitors were very satisfied.

The next day the well-grassed pitch, with a hint of variable bounce for good measure, proved just as friendly for Lillee and Max Walker. The procession of batsmen was barely interrupted. The crowd bayed their support for Lillee, chanting as he ran in. John Arlott, sent to Australia by the BBC for the first time in a quarter of a century, caught the mood, describing the seagulls on the outfield "standing in line, like vultures for Lillee".

Derek Randall, the endearingly eccentric Nottingham-shire batsman who had made his debut during the tour of India, responded to one Lillee bouncer that whistled past him by taking his cap off to the bowler, but Lillee's response was to have him caught behind next ball.

Lillee finished with six for 26; Walker was an admirable accomplice, picking up four wickets. England were all out after lunch for 95, and after only a day-and-a-half of the match Australia were starting their second innings 43 runs ahead. The Queen's visit to the match was scheduled for the final day and now worried officials started to investigate the possibility of bringing that forward.

The leg-spinner, Kerry O'Keeffe, was Ian Davis' opening partner in place of the injured McCosker, but after

the first-wicket stand had increased that lead by 33, Old and Lever struck back to have Australia 53 for 3. Davis was joined by the laconic Doug Walters and they ensured no further alarms that evening, seeing the hundred up before the close of the second day.

At last, on the third day, the batsmen began to hold sway. Davis and Walters continued their partnership until they added 79. After Greig had had Davis caught behind for 68, Walters was joined by Australia's Test debutant David Hookes, a 21-year-old trainee P.E. teacher from Adelaide, who had come into the game with a reputation for rapid scoring. He did not disappoint. Five consecutive balls from Tony Greig went for four, in all directions. He was out in the next over, caught at short leg off Underwood for 56 made from 59 balls.

Walters went for 66, but Rod Marsh shrugged off his recent poor batting form with some clean hitting of his own – nine fours before the close, to reach 95 not out. By then, Australia had ensured that England would need in excess of 400 to win. To help them get to that powerful position, Rick McCosker, his broken jaw bandaged, had returned and was himself 17 not out in the score of 387 for 8. He went on to make a heroic 25 next day, seeing Marsh to his hundred, before Old claimed him as his fourth wicket.

Not long after his departure, an hour into the fourth day, Chappell declared at 419 for 9, with Marsh 110 not

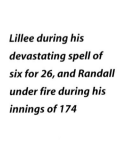

Lillee during his devastating spell of six for 26, and Randall under fire during his innings of 174

out. England had been set an improbable 463 to win and left ten hours and fifty minutes to do it in.

Bob Woolmer and Mike Brearley had put on 28 when Walker struck, having Woolmer LBW for 12.

Derek Randall walked down the long, shallow slope between the seating in front of the dressing room and on to the huge circular playing area of the MCG. It was an untidy walk out to bat. It had the air of the cheeky school-boy trying to pretend to his master that he has not really been raiding the school tuck shop. The England innings, and indeed the whole Test match, could so easily now be about to subside in ignominy, but soon Randall was playing some attacking shots against Max Walker and heartening the old England players in the stands.

Walker gave way to Lillee. Randall was spoiling the Australian party. In one eight-ball over, Lillee banged six of

them in short – there was no restriction on numbers of bouncers at this time, provided the intimidation law was followed – and Randall's reply was to take 12 off the over.

Brearley was the rock of defence; Randall the rapier of attack. Together they added 85 in a little over two hours before Lillee had Brearley LBW for 43. Dennis Amiss was no less resolute, despite offering an early chance to short leg, and the third-wicket stand, too, started to blossom.

Randall's half-century came up from 88 balls and by the time the stumps were drawn at the end of a fourth day that many had felt would not be reached by this Test, he had exposed the reliance Australia were placing on Lillee and Walker, especially after Gary Gilmour had had to withdraw injured. He was 87 not out and had rekindled a fighting spirit in the England dressing room.

Tony Greig confirmed the excitement, declaring: "We

Randall with his Man of the Match award and, right, clashing with Greg Chappell. But it was Lillee who was chaired from the field in triumph by Gary Cosier and Greg Chappell after taking 11 wickets in the match

will now fight to the death." There was excitement, too, on the other side of the world. BBC Radio had only been carrying commentary on the last session of play each day, but now they decided to take the whole of the last day.

Was it just possible that, at 191 for 2, England could give this historic Test match a historic result? They would now need 272 more with eight wickets in hand – and that sounded much less daunting.

There were twelve overs to go before the new ball became due on the final morning, but there was still a fiery burst from Lillee in advance of that. However, Randall was equal to it. He pulled Lillee to square leg, late cut him past third man and then flicked him down to fine leg to bring up his first Test hundred in his first Test against Australia.

The phlegmatic Amiss was just the man to give a calming word, lest the excitement go to the enthusiastic Randall's head. They took their third-wicket partnership to

166. The target was now less than 200 runs away. Thousands of miles away, radio listeners under the bedclothes were beginning to allow themselves to believe in miracles. But then Chappell, having had to call on his own gentle medium pace, got one to keep low and bowl Amiss for 64.

Keith Fletcher's stay was brief. Lillee had him caught behind for 1. It was 290 for 4 as Greig joined Randall.

He was certainly one to relish Randall's jousts with Lillee. Randall ducked under one bouncer and, as he had the previous day, removed his cap to the bowler. Floored by another bouncer, he performed a backward somersault. To a piece of caustic advice from Lillee, he cupped an ear, asking him to repeat it. There was something charming about the eccentric Randall that appeared to mute Lillee's fury rather than exacerbate it, as Greig himself had done two-and-a-half years before.

The shot of the day was a flat pull off Lillee that

travelled to the midwicket boundary like a shell. But then, with his score 161, Randall got an edge to a ball from Greg Chappell. Marsh tumbled to take the low catch and umpire Tom Brooks raised his finger above his head.

The glorious innings was over – or was it? There was Marsh running down the pitch to tell his captain and then the umpire that he had not taken the catch cleanly. Randall, head down and making for the dressing room, was recalled. It was a moment of sportsmanship thoroughly in keeping with the occasion.

Chappell may not have taken that wicket, but he had put the brake on England's rush to glory. Just before tea he risked the use of O'Keeffe, the leg spinner, and immediately Randall was snapped up with a splendid catch at short leg. He had made 174 and exhilarated all who had seen him.

He wandered off, almost apologetically, so apparently disorientated by the reception he was getting that he took the wrong gate off the field and found himself walking up the approach to the Royal Box. Realising his mistake rather late, he stopped, doffed his cap and bowed to the Queen and departed through the members' seating to the dressing room.

England did not, after Randall, really look as if they would get to their target. Greig fell in similar manner to Randall for 41 and Knott played some fine attacking shots when Lillee returned to try to polish off the innings.

The great fast bowler was giving it his all, bowling as quickly as at any time in the match. He got Old caught at slip and bowled Underwood. O'Keeffe had Lever LBW and then, as the shadows lengthened at the end of a match that had not looked likely to go beyond three days, he had Knott LBW for 42.

Australia had won by 45 runs – exactly the same result they had achieved 100 years before. Lillee had taken eleven wickets in the match, but as he was chaired from the field, he found he had been pipped for the man-of-the-match award by the cheeky lad from Notts, Derek Randall.

Cricket seemed to be at the height of popularity and, while the on-the-field drama was watched by the cricketing world, more far-reaching events were taking place in Melbourne hotel bedrooms, as the secret recruitment was under way for what would explode in public in a few months' time as the Packer circus of World Series Cricket.

Australia v England

MCG, Melbourne, Australia
England won the toss and fielded

12.3.1977 - 17.3.1977
Australia won by 45 runs

Australia	1st innings		2nd innings	
I.C.Davis	lbw b Lever	5	c Knott b Greig	68
R.B.McCosker	b Willis	4	(10) c Greig b Old	25
G.J.Cosier	c Fletcher b Lever	10	(4) c Knott b Lever	4
*G.S.Chappell	b Underwood	40	(3) b Old	2
D.W.Hookes	c Greig b Old	17	(6) c Fletcher b Underwood	56
K.D.Walters	c Greig b Willis	4	(5) c Knott b Greig	66
+R.W.Marsh	c Knott b Old	28	not out	110
G.J.Gilmour	c Greig b Old	4	b Lever	16
K.J.O'Keeffe	c Brearley b Underwood	0	(2) c Willis b Old	14
D.K.Lillee	not out	10	(9) c Amiss b Old	25
M.H.N.Walker	b Underwood	2	not out	8
Extras	(b-4, lb-2, w-0, nb-8)	14	(b-0, lb-10, w-0, nb-15)	25
TOTAL	(all out)	138	(for 9 wickets declared)	419

Fall of Wickets 1-11 2-13 3-23 4-45 5-51 1-33 2-40 3-53 4-132 5-187
6-102 7-114 8-117 9-136 10-138 6-244 7-277 8-353 9-407

Bowling Analysis	O	M	R	W	O	M	R	W
J.K.Lever	12	1	36	2	21	1	95	2
R.G.D.Willis	8	0	33	2	22	0	91	0
C.M.Old	12	4	39	3	27.6	2	104	4
D.L.Underwood	11.6	2	16	3	12	2	38	1
A.W.Greig	14	3	66	2				

England	1st innings		2nd innings	
R.A.Woolmer	c Chappell b Lillee	9	lbw b Walker	12
J.M.Brearley	c Hookes b Lillee	12	lbw b Lillee	43
D.L.Underwood	c Chappell b Walker	7	(10) b Lillee	7
D.W.Randall	c Marsh b Lillee	4	(3) c Cosier b O'Keeffe	174
D.L.Amiss	c O'Keeffe b Walker	4	(4) b Chappell	64
K.W.R.Fletcher	c Marsh b Walker	4	(5) c Marsh b Lillee	1
*A.W.Greig	b Walker	18	(6)c Cosier b O'Keeffe	41
+A.P.E.Knott	lbw b Lillee	15	(7) lbw b Lillee	42
C.M.Old	c Marsh b Lillee	3	(8) c Chappell b Lillee	2
J.K.Lever	c Marsh b Lillee	11	(9) lbw b O'Keeffe	4
R.G.D.Willis	not out	1	not out	5
Extras	(b-2, lb-2, w-1, nb-2)	7	(b-8, lb-4, w-3, nb-7)	22
TOTAL	(all out)	95	(all out)	417

Fall of Wickets 1-19 2-30 3-34 4-40 5-40 1-28 2-113 3-279 4-290 5-346
6-61 7-65 8-78 9-86 10-95 6-369 7-380 8-385 9-410 10-417

Bowling Analysis	O	M	R	W	O	M	R	W
D.K.Lillee	13.3	2	26	6	34.4	7	139	5
M.H.N.Walker	15	3	54	4	22	4	83	1
K.J.O'Keeffe	1	0	4	0	33	6	108	3
G.J.Gilmour	5	3	4	0	4	0	29	0
G.S.Chappell					16	7	29	1
K.D.Walters					3	2	7	0

Umpires: T.F.Brooks, M.G.O'Connell   Man of the Match: D.K.Randall

NASSER HUSSAIN'S ANALYSIS

'No helmet on, doffing his cap to one of the world's fastest bowlers – sheer cheek'

'Tactically or psychologically, it's not easy for the opposition to work out how to play against someone like that.'

Right: Randall finds another novel way to avoid a Lillee bouncer

Like Jack Russell, Derek Randall's tics and quirky mannerisms helped him to survive in Test cricket. There was a madness about Randall which saw him through all the pressure situations.

He was a quite phenomenal cricketer. They talk about David Gower's timing of the ball but I've never seen anything to match Randall. When Essex played Nottinghamshire I used to be fielding in the covers and he would push it past me and I would turn to chase it and find that it had gone.

This battle typified him. He was a good player of quick bowling, with a lot of bottle. No helmet on, doffing his cap to one of the world's fastest bowlers – sheer cheek. Everyone saw Randall as a nutter and I think that's why he got away with it.

Tactically or psychologically, it's not easy for the opposition to work out how to play against someone like that: whether to go along with his craziness or to give him a hard time. Jack always argues that if you're nice to him it annoys the hell out of him and he would rather that you had a go at him.

At Essex we've tried every approach with Jack. First, the polite "Good morning, Robert" – because his real name is

NASSER HUSSAIN'S ANALYSIS

'They talk about David Gower's timing of the ball but I've never seen anything to match Randall.'

'Lillee gave Randall a load of verbals as well as bouncers, and Randall's infuriating response was: Come on, give me more of the same…'

Robert Russell – "have you had a nice cup of tea this morning?" But that doesn't seem to work, so then we've tried sledging him, telling him to stop mucking about and get on with the game. The trouble is, that just makes him behave even more eccentrically.

Whether the Australians tried that with Randall, I just don't know. Lillee gave Randall a load of verbals as well as bouncers, and Randall's infuriating response was: "Come on, give me more of the same." That's the trouble with the mad ones – they've always got a comeback.

BRIAN CLOSE
V
WES HALL

THE PROTAGONISTS

Brian Close
(Yorkshire & England)
Aged 32. Playing his
ninth Test, having been
the youngest player to
represent England,
aged 18 in 1949.
After batting between
2 and 9 in the order in
his first eight Tests,
spread over 14 years,
had made 267 runs, but
became England
captain in 1966.

Wes Hall
(Barbados & West Indies)
Aged 25. Playing his
25th Test, starting with
116 wickets. After
retirement, with 192
wickets from 48 Tests,
he became a Senator in
the Barbados
parliament.

BRIAN CLOSE

WES HALL

The harder they come

Second Test • Lord's • June 25, 1963

*The reggae movie The Harder They Come was a celebration of West Indian tough guys –
but it could just as easily have been the catchphrase of a certain tough guy from Yorkshire.
Brian Close's suicidal technique for facing fast bowling required nerves of steel and a skull
made of concrete: "You bowl 'em, I'll head 'em…" Wes Hall was only too pleased to oblige*

Wisden, which is not given to exaggeration, records this celebrated Lord's Test as "one of the most dramatic Test Matches ever to be played in England". There were so many facets to the drama. Cavalier batting by Dexter, Hunte against Trueman and the Yorkshireman's response, Butcher's courageous response to personal tragedy, Cowdrey coming out with his arm in plaster … and, amongst it all, Brian Close taking on Wes Hall.

The West Indies had overwhelmed England in the First Test at Old Trafford. Conrad Hunte had made a big hundred and there had been runs, too, from Rohan

Kanhai, Gary Sobers and Frank Worrell. The feared duo of Hall and Charlie Griffith had softened England up with pace and Lance Gibbs had taken eleven wickets with his off spin.

For the Lord's Test, the England selectors had strengthened the batting by bringing in Jim Parks to keep wicket in place of Keith Andrew and, more surprisingly, Derek Shackleton to replace Brian Statham.

The drama of the Test started in its first over. Conrad Hunte took a boundary off each of Fred Trueman's first

'Colin Cowdrey, with his arm in plaster, was watching anxiously from the Lord's dressing room balcony...'

three balls, but it was Trueman who had the last laugh, taking five for 64 on that first day, including Hunte for 44 and the top scorer, Kanhai, for 73. Trueman finished with six for 100 when the West Indies were all out on the second morning for 301. Shackleton, playing his first Test for nearly 12 years, had bowled fifty overs to take three for 93.

In the brief period before lunch, the formidable Charlie Griffith removed both openers with only twenty runs scored. The afternoon, though, belonged to Ted Dexter.

Hard cases: Brian Close – a left-handed batsman who bowled with both left and right hands – and Wes Hall, who only knew one way to bowl. Fast...

The West Indian captain Frank Worrell was bowled by Trueman for nought after Conrad Hunte (right) had taken boundaries off Fred's first three balls. Centre: Colin Cowdrey drops his bat as a ball from Wes Hall breaks his arm

He drove, cut and hooked the fastest that Hall and Griffith could send down with, in the words of John Arlott's commentary at the time, "dignity and something near majesty". He made 70 from 75 balls, with ten fours, the runs coming out of 100 scored while he was in. Ken Barrington, who shared a third-wicket stand of 82 with him, contributed only 20 to it. When Dexter was LBW to Sobers at 102 for 3, a packed Lord's gave him a standing ovation.

Barrington went on to make 80, and Fred Titmus was 52 not out when England were all out on Saturday morning for 297, only four runs behind. When the West Indies went to lunch at 15 for 2, the match was on a knife edge. After the interval Basil Butcher, who had received news from home that morning that his wife had suffered a miscarriage, came in and, despite losing Kanhai, Sobers and Joe Solomon cheaply, stroked his way to a century. With his captain, Frank Worrell, he had taken the score from 104 when the fifth wicket fell to a position of strength at 214 for 5 at the close.

On the Monday morning that situation, so promising for the West Indies, rapidly declined as the last five wickets fell to Trueman and Shackleton in 25 minutes. Butcher was ninth out for 133 and they were all out for 229. Trueman had taken five for 52 and Shackleton four for 72.

England were set the task of making 234 – the highest total yet to win a Lord's Test. Time was not, on the face of it, a problem. As Micky Stewart and John Edrich came out to open, they were only 35 minutes into the fourth day, but dark clouds were lowering and would cause two breaks in play and an early finish.

The score was 15 when Edrich was caught behind down the leg side, which brought in Dexter to an acclaim that echoed his first-innings heroics. But Worrell did not this time give him the chance to take on the fast bowlers, bringing Gibbs on. It was a stroke of genius, as the off-spinner bowled the England captain for 2. By that time, too, Stewart had ducked to a Hall bouncer, but "left the periscope up" as he did so and was caught in the slips off the bat handle.

So Colin Cowdrey joined Ken Barrington at 31 for 3.

Now the West Indies were very definitely favourites. Having been grateful to make it into the pavilion for lunch, Barrington and Cowdrey were much more assured in the afternoon. Hall, determined to force home the advantage as the stand began to pull England round, was bowling out of the dark background of the pavilion at furious pace and often fearfully short.

With the score at 72 for 3, he produced a rapid delivery that reared at Cowdrey and struck him on the left forearm. Immediately the loud crack of bone told everyone what the consequence was. Cowdrey retired hurt, his arm broken. England were as good as four wickets down now, as Brian Close came in in worsening light.

The Yorkshireman had a reputation as a tough player, but the tactic he adopted now was bizarre. Despite what had just happened to Cowdrey, he decided to keep Hall out at all costs. His technique to the paceman's sharply lifting deliveries was to allow them to hit him on the body, thrusting his chest out to take the bruise rather than risk fending one away to a close fielder's waiting hands.

Close made little attempt to score, but settled, with apparently insane bravery, for soaking up the threat. And Hall at last, after a long spell, was spent. He was replaced by Charlie Griffith – menacing enough himself, as he strove to find the perfect yorker.

The light deteriorated still further and brought the players off the field twice, either side of a tea-interval visit from the Queen, and eventually England were grateful to get through to a finish an hour-and-three-quarters early with no more losses. They would start the last day at 116 for 3 – effectively four – needing another 118 to win.

Poor light and drizzle next morning threatened to ruin everyone's anticipation of a tense finish. No play was possible until after lunch and the weather had kept the crowd down. Lance Gibbs opened proceedings from the Nursery End, giving way to Griffith after one over, and inevitably Hall was given the wind at his back from the Pavilion End. Of fourteen overs that he bowled in that spell before tea, Close took eleven of them, still content to receive blows on the body in defence of his wicket, presenting a proud chest to absorb all that the tall Barbadian could hurl at him.

Barrington, meanwhile, was looking less certain than he had the day before and fell to a catch behind the wicket as he tried to cut Griffith. He had made 60 and now it was 130 for 4. Only 14 runs had come from the first thirteen overs bowled in the day, and an hour before tea 104 more runs were needed to win.

Jim Parks got the scoreboard moving again with some choice cover drives, which seemed to encourage Close to start to employ his bat against the fast bowlers. But an inswinger to Parks kept low and he was LBW for 17. It was 158 for 5. The approach of the new batsman, Fred Titmus, was to push quick singles and England went to tea at 171 for 5, with the target 63 runs away.

The Close who returned after the interval was in a

Ted Dexter introduces the Queen to Messrs Cowdrey, Trueman, Parks and Barrington, while a West Indian supporter makes sure no one nicks his beer

'I made Wes lose his rag. In he came, all power and fire and fury, and just as he was getting into his delivery stride he saw me coming towards him. His eyes popped like chapel hat-pegs.'

BRIAN CLOSE IN HIS AUTOBIOGRAPHY, 'I DON'T BRUISE EASILY'

more aggressive frame of mind. Now the winning line was almost in sight and three runs an over would get them there. Hall continued, as he had all afternoon, from the Pavilion End and now, when he bowled short, Close was having a go, hooking to fine leg for four and then seeing Butcher run round to cut off another boundary. Griffith and Gibbs, alternating at the other end, also suffered.

Another hook off Hall brought up Close's fifty. England were rushing towards victory, with Titmus playing the ideal foil to the belligerent Close.

The 200 came up, but at 203 Titmus was caught at short leg off Hall for 11. When Trueman edged his first ball to the wicketkeeper, England's cause was again in the hazard at 203 for 7.

Cowdrey, with his arm in plaster, was watching anxiously from the dressing room balcony.

Out on the pitch, Close was still continuing to take the attack to the opposition although there were effectively now only two wickets in hand.

Hall was bathed in sweat, his shirt limp and the crucifix round his neck bouncing on a glistening chest as he pounded in fully 40 yards every ball.

Brian Close later said that he did not try to watch the paceman until he was almost into his delivery stride, but Hall on one marathon run-in pulled up in amazement. There was this foolhardy Yorkshireman at the other end advancing down the wicket to him – the fastest bowler in the world. It took a consoling word from his captain, Frank Worrell, to get the big man back to his mark to try again.

That did not put Close off. He continued to walk

down the wicket to Hall and Griffith and he continued to prosper. Now only 15 runs were needed. Worrell did not dare take the new ball for fear that it might leave the bat more quickly, but England were surely favourites. But then Close advanced once too often to Griffith, got a faint bottom edge and was caught behind. He had made 70 from 198 balls, very nearly half of them from Wes Hall, against whose bowling he had hit five of his eight boundaries.

Close's continued presence would surely have brought an England win, but now, at 219 for 8, it looked more difficult.

Derek Shackleton and David Allen were the batsmen, and in the dressing room Colin Cowdrey had changed and padded up, and was practising batting left-handed. There were five overs left to score those 15 runs and three of them would be bowled by Hall.

Still, after twenty overs in the day unchanged, the man from Barbados was bowling frighteningly fast, just short of a length, with close fielders lurking to snap up what might be the final wicket.

The ninth-wicket pair added six in four overs, so that they needed eight from the last. Hall was to bowl it. Shackleton took a single from the second ball and Allen one from the third. A bye was attempted to Deryck Murray, the keeper, but Shackleton was late setting off for the bowler's end and found himself being out-sprinted by Worrell. He was run out for four. It was 228 for 9.

Six runs were needed and two balls remained. All eyes were on the door leading out of the Long Room. And from it emerged Colin Cowdrey, his left forearm in a cast. With Cowdrey at the non-striker's end, Allen opted for safety

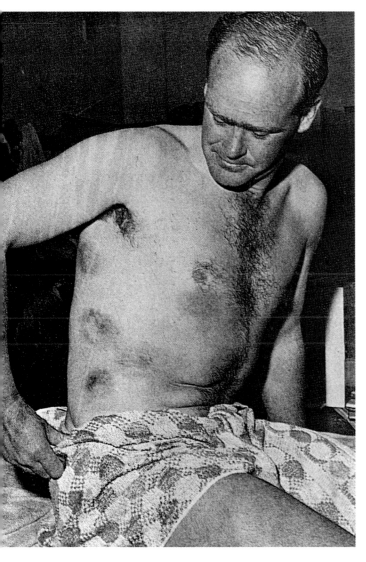

*After his relentless battering by Wes Hall and Charlie Griffith,
Brian Close shows the scars of battle*

England v West Indies

Lords, London, England
West Indies won the toss and batted

20.6.1963 - 25.6.1963
Match Drawn

West Indies	1st innings		2nd innings	
C.C.Hunte	c Close b Trueman	44	c Cowdrey b Shackleton	7
E.D.A.StJ.McMorris	lbw b Trueman	16	c Cowdrey b Trueman	8
G.StA.Sobers	c Cowdrey b Allen	42	(5) c Parks b Trueman	8
R.B.Kanhai	c Edrich b Trueman	73	(3) c Cowdrey b Shackleton	21
B.F.Butcher	c Barrington b Trueman	14	(4) lbw b Shackleton	133
J.S.Solomon	lbw b Shackleton	56	c Stewart b Allen	5
*F.M.M.Worrell	b Trueman	0	c Stewart b Trueman	33
+D.L.Murray	c Cowdrey b Trueman	20	c Parks b Trueman	2
W.W.Hall	not out	25	c Parks b Trueman	2
C.C.Griffith	c Cowdrey b Shackleton	0	b Shackleton	1
L.R.Gibbs	c Stewart b Shackleton	0	not out	1
Extras	(b-10, lb-1, w-0, nb-0)	11	(b-5, lb-2, w-0, nb-1)	8
TOTAL	(all out)	301	(all out)	229

Fall of Wickets	1-51	2-64	3-127	4-145	5-219	1-15	2-15	3-64	4-84	5-104
	6-219	7-263	8-297	9-297	10-301	6-214	7-224	8-226	9-228	10-229

Bowling Analysis	O	M	R	W	O	M	R	W
F.S.Trueman	44	16	100	6	26	9	52	5
D.Shackleton	50.2	22	93	3	34	14	72	4
E.R.Dexter	20	6	41	0				
D.B.Close	9	3	21	0				
D.A.Allen	10	3	35	1	21	7	50	1
F.J.Titmus	17	3	47	0				

England	1st innings		2nd innings	
M.J.Stewart	c Kanhai b Griffith	2	c Solomon b Hall	17
J.H.Edrich	c Murray b Griffith	0	c Murray b Hall	8
*E.R.Dexter	lbw b Sobers	70	b Gibbs	2
K.F.Barrington	c Sobers b Worrell	80	c Murray b Griffith	60
M.C.Cowdrey	b Gibbs	4	not out	19
D.B.Close	c Murray b Griffith	9	c Murray b Griffith	70
+J.M.Parks	b Worrell	35	lbw b Griffith	17
F.J.Titmus	not out	52	c McMorris b Hall	11
F.S.Trueman	b Hall	10	c Murray b Hall	0
D.A.Allen	lbw b Griffith	2	not out	4
D.Shackleton	b Griffith	8	run out	4
Extras	(b-8, lb-8, w-0, nb-9)	25	(b-5, lb-8, w-0, nb-3)	16
TOTAL	(all out)	297	(for 9 wickets)	228

Fall of Wickets	1-2	2-20	3-102	4-115	5-151	1-15	2-27	3-31	4-130	5-158
	6-206	7-235	8-271	9-274	10-297	6-203	7-203	8-219	9-228	

Bowling Analysis	O	M	R	W	O	M	R	W
W.W.Hall	18	2	65	1	40	9	93	4
C.C.Griffith	26	6	91	5	30	7	59	3
G.StA.Sobers	18	4	45	1	4	1	4	0
L.R.Gibbs	27	9	59	1	17	7	56	1
F.M.M.Worrell	13	6	12	2				

Umpires: J.S.Butler, W.E.Phillipson

and managed to keep out Hall's last two balls for a draw. In the dressing room in the aftermath Brian Close displayed his bruises – badges of courage – to the photographers and maybe first planted the thoughts of the title of his subsequent autobiography, *I Don't Bruise Easily*.

Fred Trueman was to bowl England to victory at Edgbaston, but the West Indies won the last two Tests to take the series 3-1.

NASSER HUSSAIN'S ANALYSIS

'Yorkshire grit taken to the extreme'

Wes Hall would have been as fast as anything we face now. These days we all wear chest pads and lots of other protection, because there are certain parts of the body where if you get hit you know about it – and the ribs are a very, very sore area. So it must have been quite painful.

This is a story that is often told to players of my generation. When I broke my finger at Lord's in 1999 and didn't go out to bat, I inevitably got a letter saying: "Brian Close wouldn't have done that." This is the same Test match where Cowdrey came in to bat with his arm in plaster, and I think I got that letter as well. Maybe they were tougher back then…

But what amuses me is that he posed for the photos afterwards. Nowadays we get the bruises and nobody knows about it, so I'd put him

down as a show-off, to be honest. Especially after that article where he said the current England team should all be hung, drawn and quartered…

Seriously, though, this was an example of Yorkshire grit taken to the extreme. It's interesting to note that Close scored 70 rather than 100 or 150, and yet people still talk about it 40 years later. It just shows that there are certain types of innings and attitudes that the British public will always love to see. This man had the guts to walk down the wicket to Wes Hall and take it on the chest, and consequently that innings is remembered more than if he had played in an orthodox way and got 150.

It's amazing to think that, 13 years later, Close was recalled for the Old Trafford Test at the age of 45 to face the same kind of bombardment at the hands of Andy Roberts, Wayne Daniel

NASSER HUSSAIN'S ANALYSIS

'There are certain parts of the body where if you get hit you know about it – and the ribs are a very, very sore area.'

and Michael Holding. In the pictures of that innings, he's not wearing a cap – and you could swear he was deliberately trying to head the ball into touch. It's not a technique I would advocate myself. But fair's fair, Brian, I have to admit it: you were a real tough cookie.

• Nasser Hussain did, of course, play two Test matches against Ambrose, Marshall & Co in the West Indies in 1990 with a broken wrist – Ed.

Hall in full flight … and the famous 'heading-the-ball-into-touch' picture of Brian Close

'YOU AND ME. OUTSIDE. NOW!'

'You and me. Outside. Now!'

ATHERTON V **DONALD** · **TRENT BRIDGE** · **1998**

GATTING V **SHAKOOR RANA** · **FAISALABAD** · **1987**

Opposite: Michael Atherton and Allan Donald. Good pals. But not on this day…
This page: Allan Donald; and Mike Gatting and Shakoor Rana. Not pals at all…

MICHAEL ATHERTON
V
ALLAN DONALD

THE PROTAGONISTS

Michael Atherton

(Lancashire & England)
Aged 30. Had given up
the England captaincy
after the last Test in the
West Indies in March.
Playing his 83rd Test
match, having
previously made 5,762
runs with 12 centuries.

Allan Donald

*(Free State
& South Africa)*
Aged 31. One of the
fastest bowlers in the
world – nicknamed
White Lightning.
Playing his 46th Test,
having previously taken
223 wickets.

MICHAEL ATHERTON

ALLAN DONALD

High Noon in Nottingham

Third Test · Trent Bridge · July 26, 1998

This is what happens when an immovable object sticks itself in the way of an irresistible force. Allan Donald was arguably the world's most explosive bowler. Michael Atherton was undoubtedly the world's most obstinate batsman. No one who saw this furious exchange will ever forget it ... including Nasser Hussain, who just happened to be batting with Atherton at the time

They had, of course, had battles before. This was a new encounter in a long campaign. Allan Donald certainly would not have forgotten the hours he bowled at Michael Atherton at the Wanderers ground in Johannesburg towards the end of 1995. Then, as now, a Test match and possibly even a series hung on the outcome.

Then, Atherton had been England's captain, a position he had resigned in the aftermath of defeat in the West Indies in 1997/98. Then, Atherton had had to hold on in an innings of monumental concentration to save a match. This was more red-blooded. Here, the winner would take all.

Earlier in the summer of 1998, the First Test at

'YOU AND ME. OUTSIDE. NOW!'

Edgbaston had been fascinatingly poised. England had finished the fourth day 289 ahead with two second-innings wickets in hand. South Africa would probably need 300 in two-and-a-half sessions to win. But the last word went to the weather, with not a ball bowled on the final day.

Atherton had made a century there before being bowled by Donald. At Lord's, Donald had him caught at slip off a lifter for nought. England's Lord's bogey struck and South Africa won by ten wickets.

At Old Trafford, the tourists made 552 for 5 declared and, for the second successive Test, made England follow on. They had five-and-a-half sessions to bat and Atherton's

Donald suggests that Atherton could be out. The batsman – and his partner Nasser Hussain – decide to await the umpire's verdict...

89 occupied over half of that. Donald's six wickets – none of them Atherton's – left the last pair fighting to avert an innings defeat, and it was Angus Fraser who kept Donald and the new ball at bay to save the match.

So the five-match series was still one-nil to South Africa when the teams arrived in Nottingham for the Fourth Test. Alec Stewart's decision to put the visitors in was possibly influenced by apprehension of what Donald and Pollock might make of a greenish-looking pitch. Five wickets down before 200 was on the board just about justified the decision, but a captain's innings by Hansie Cronje restored South Africa's fortunes. His 126 took him into the second day before he became Fraser's fifth victim. South Africa were all out just before lunch on the second day for 374.

Mike Atherton had already had three opening partners in the series, because of an injury to Mark Butcher. But Butcher was back now and together they made a challenging reply, putting on 145 for the first wicket. Donald had them both, Atherton caught behind for 58 and Butcher LBW for 75, in successive overs. The innings rather fell away after that, Mark Ramprakash having to bat with the

'I felt in my bones the game would be decided in the next few overs. I had to get the adrenalin flowing. I told Hansie Cronje that the sparks were going to fly.'

ALLAN DONALD,
'WHITE LIGHTNING'

tail in familiar style to be 67 not out when the end came at tea on the third day – all out for 336. Allan Donald had taken five wickets.

On a heady Saturday afternoon, under the gaze of the newly-opened Radcliffe Road Stand, the England bowlers set about trying to prevent South Africa building too much on that slender lead of 38. Gough had a wicket in the first over, and Fraser and Cork claimed one each before the innings was an hour old. South Africa were reeling at 21 for 3. By the end of the third day, though, captain Cronje was again at the helm and the lead had grown to 130.

On Sunday, Angus Fraser and Dominic Cork bowled England back into the match, Cork taking four for 60 and Fraser his tenth wicket of the match, with five for 62. With Cronje out for 67, South Africa were dismissed for 208. England needed 247 to square the series with a day-and-a-half to go. It may not have seemed much, but England's history of batting collapses was not encouraging.

As early as the third over, there should have been a run-out to separate the openers, as Atherton ran a ball from Donald to the electric Rhodes at backward point. Atherton made as if to run and, as he changed his mind about the wisdom of that, Butcher arrived in his crease. With apparently no hope, Atherton set off for the bowler's end, but unaccountably Rhodes' throw was whipped in to the wrong end and Atherton was home with an eventful single.

Maybe inflamed by that missed chance, Donald was working up the kind of speed that brought him his nickname of White Lightning. As he pushed towards 90mph, the crowd monitored every new advance on the display of the speed gun read-outs. A fine inside edge on to the pad spared Atherton in a huge shout for LBW from Donald, then a Pollock bouncer flew off his shoulder to slip, where Cullinan loudly claimed the catch. And Pollock it was who made the breakthrough, when Butcher got an outside edge to the wicketkeeper for 22, when the score was 40.

That brought in Nasser Hussain, who had played representative cricket with Atherton since they were teenagers. There were 27 overs of the day still to go. Cronje experimented with some overs of Paul Adams' eccentric left-arm spin, but the crunch would surely come with the return of Donald for a serious blast of speed before the close.

> '*Elsewhere, parishioners were making their way peacefully to Sunday evensong, but inside the walls of Trent Bridge a war was being fought...*'

Fast it was – and short. The showdown came when Donald switched to bowling round the wicket to Atherton. His first lightning delivery from that angle produced what appeared to be a glance off Atherton's glove to Mark Boucher behind the wicket. Atherton, on 27, stood his ground as the South Africans went into wild celebration.

But an impassive umpire Steve Dunne was unmoved. The fielding team were aghast. There was much eyeballing between bowler and batsman, and several hostile glares at the New Zealand umpire.

When Donald finally came in to bowl the next ball, his mood was not greatly improved by the sight of a rapid, full-length delivery flying to the fine-leg boundary off Atherton's inside edge, to take the score to 86 for 1.

Atherton could not have been surprised by the bouncer that he allowed to whistle over his shoulder next ball. Donald followed through to voice an opinion in the face of the impassive batsman, who simply stared levelly back at

the bowler through the grille of his helmet.

There was another terse comment from Donald after another short ball had finished the hostile over.

Elsewhere, parishioners were making their way peacefully to Sunday evensong, but inside the walls of Trent Bridge a war was being fought between a furious tornado from Bloemfontein and a laconic, cussed Lancastrian. No onlooker could take his eyes off the raw-boned contest.

Another Donald bouncer induced Atherton to hook high over the square-leg fielder for four – Adams, the far from lofty man in that position, back-pedalling furiously as the ball appeared to hang tantalisingly above him.

Nasser Hussain, a close spectator at the furious duel, still had to accept his share. There was a big appeal from Boucher and Donald as a ball flicked his trousers and, when at last Donald found the edge of his bat, it was only to see Boucher drop the chance.

Donald's extraordinary, elemental cry of anguish could surely have been heard on the High Veldt.

Later on, witnesses might discuss the law's interpretation of intimidatory bowling, but for now it had the fascination of the ring. It was in everyone's mind that the issue would be decided that evening – and when the umpires finally did call time, it was the battered

Donald wheels away in frustration as Atherton stands firm

*Allan Donald emotes;
Mike Atherton hooks;
and Nasser Hussain
and Donald engage in
a balletic pas de deux
during the battle of
Trent Bridge 1998*

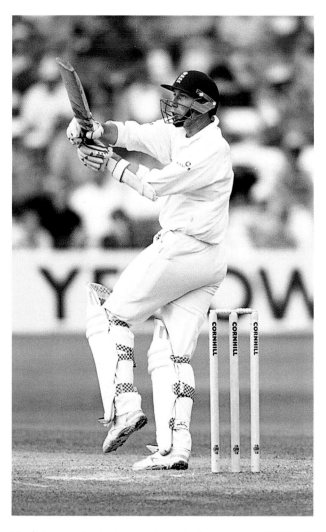

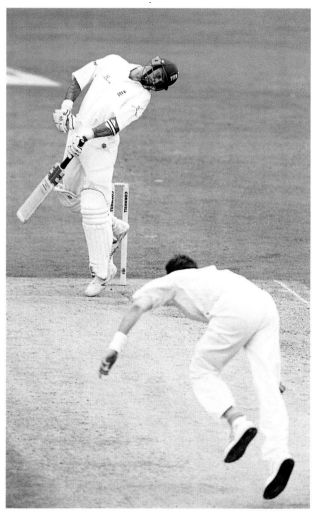

Englishmen who had come through the storm. At 108 for 1, they would need 139 next day to win.

The achievement of that target was not, of course, a foregone conclusion and an uncharacteristically large fifth-day crowd of 11,000 came in expectation of further stern battle, but after Donald's opening burst it seemed more straightforward. The 150 partnership was reached just before lunch. Donald at last got his wicket – Hussain brilliantly caught by Kallis at slip for 58 – in the first over after the interval, with 55 still needed.

Mike Atherton had battled his way to 88 by then and the swashbuckling approach of his captain as he now came to the crease must have given him cause for a wry smile. In

two dozen balls Stewart had rattled up 38, with eight boundaries, a state of affairs that was now threatening Atherton's chance of a century.

Stewart offered to help him get there, but was told just to get on with winning it. This was a grown-up game and, when a single off the last ball of one over and a boundary in the next would have given Atherton both his hundred and the victory, typically he ran three to take himself to 98 and England to an eight-wicket win.

A fortnight later, not without more umpiring contro-versy, England had won the final Test at Headingley and in the space of three weeks had converted a one-nil deficit to a series win. The South Africans could scarcely believe it.

England v South Africa

Trent Bridge, Nottingham, England
England won the toss and fielded

23.7.1998 - 27.7.1998
England won by 8 runs

South Africa	1st innings		2nd innings	
G.Kirsten	b Gough	7	lbw b Fraser	6
G.F.J.Liebenberg	c Stewart b Gough	13	lbw b Gough	0
J.H.Kallis	c Stewart b Flintoff	47	c Stewart b Cork	11
D.J.Cullinan	c Ramprakash b Fraser	30	c Ramprakash b Fraser	56
*W.J.Cronje	c Hick b Fraser	126	c Stewart b Cork	67
J.N.Rhodes	lbw b Fraser	24	c Stewart b Cork	2
S.M.Pollock	c Stewart b Fraser	50	c Stewart b Cork	7
+M.V.Boucher	lbw b Fraser	4	c Hussain b Fraser	35
S.Elworthy	c Ramprakash b Gough	48	lbw b Fraser	10
A.A.Donald	not out	4	not out	7
P.Adams	c Hick b Gough	0	c Stewart b Fraser	1
Extras	(b-9, lb-3, w-0, nb-9)	21	(b-1, lb-4, w-1, nb-0)	6
TOTAL	(all out)	**374**	(all out)	**208**

Fall of Wickets	1-21	2-26	3-68	4-147	5-196	1-3	2-17	3-21	4-119	5-122
	6-292	7-302	8-325	9-374	10-374	6-136	7-189	8-193	9-200	10-208

Bowling Analysis	O	M	R	W		O	M	R	W
D.Gough	30.2	4	116	4		16	4	56	1
D.G.Cork	17	2	65	0		20	4	59	4
A.R.C.Fraser	26	7	60	5		28.3	6	62	5
A.Flintoff	17	2	52	1		6	1	16	0
I.D.K.Salisbury	9	1	57	0		5	2	9	0
M.Butcher	4	1	12	0					

England	1st innings		2nd innings	
M.Butcher	lbw b Donald	75	c Boucher b Pollock	22
M.A.Atherton	c Boucher b Donald	58	not out	98
N.Hussain	lbw b Elworthy	22	c Kallis b Donald	58
*+A.J.Stewart	c Kirsten b Kallis	19	not out	45
M.R.Ramprakash	not out	67		
I.D.K.Salisbury	b Donald	23		
G.A.Hick	b Donald	6		
A.Flintoff	c Boucher b Kallis	17		
D.G.Cork	c Boucher b Pollock	6		
D.Gough	c Boucher b Donald	2		
A.R.C.Fraser	lbw b Pollock	7		
Extras	(b-7, lb-13, w-1, nb-13)	34	(b-2, lb-11, w-2, nb-9)	24
TOTAL	(all out)	**336**	(for 2 wickets)	**247**

Fall of Wickets	1-145	2-150	3-191	4-199	5-244	1-40	2-192
	6-254	7-285	8-302	9-307	10-336		

Bowling Analysis	O	M	R	W		O	M	R	W
A.A.Donald	33	8	109	5		23	8	56	1
S.M.Pollock	35.5	12	75	2		26	3	79	1
S.Elworthy	22	8	41	1		9	1	38	0
J.H.Kallis	28	9	60	2		13	5	26	0
P.Adams	9	2	31	0		12	4	23	0
W.J.Cronje	4	0	12	0					

Umpires: M.J.Kitchen, R.S.Dunne   **Man of the Match:** A.R.C.Fraser

Atherton celebrates a hard-fought victory to level the series

NASSER HUSSAIN'S ANALYSIS

'I knew that Atherton had escaped – and Donald would be steaming'

'Let's put it this way, if I was the umpire I would have given it out.'

This is a battle that I saw from very close quarters, because I was actually at the other end – and funnily enough, in my mind's eye it was Atherton and Hussain versus Donald and Pollock! But no one else seems to remember it that way, so never mind…

This wasn't the old flat Trent Bridge; it was a good wicket that nibbled a bit early on, then went flat and took spin, so by the fourth afternoon it wasn't a fast bowler's track at all. Even so, I think Hansie Cronje had made a slight mistake by bringing on Paul Adams soon after I came in, because I'm a reasonably good player of spin and it got me up and running.

I've known Athers since we were 11 and I like batting with him. We've also had good partnerships at Trent Bridge. So it was now a pretty good wicket and we had good vibes.

By the time Allan Donald came back on, the South Africans could see that the time had come when they had to seize the moment. If they didn't get wickets then, the game was gone. Cronje threw the ball to Donald and from the first ball of that spell on a wicket that had become very slow and flat, with an old ball, he seemed to go up two gears. He was pumped up and he was quick.

There was about an hour-and-a-half to go on the fourth day and both sides knew this was the key phase of the game. Atherton and I met in the middle and said, "Come on, we have to get through this attack and then make sure we're still here this evening."

If we had lost a wicket, then Alec Stewart would have come in under a bit of pressure with another 100-odd needed, and with our tail and our history of collapsing, that could have been the vital breakthrough. Donald would have had a rest overnight and then they would have needed only another four or five wickets.

So we knew it was crucial to stay together and they knew it was crucial to break us up.

Donald bowled at the speed of light. At first he went over the wicket and Atherton hooked him to the boundary – but not a convincing hook because of the extra pace that Donald had generated from nowhere.

The South Africans had a theory that they should bowl round the wicket to both Atherton and me, because we both move a bit to the off, giving them the possibility of a catch down the legside, and we both hook, which is slightly

Wicketkeeper Mark Boucher (second from left) triumphantly holds the ball aloft – but as Allan Donald and Paul Adams (right) anxiously look back over their shoulders, the South Africans are beginning to realise that umpire Steve Dunne doesn't quite share their enthusiam

NASSER HUSSAIN'S ANALYSIS

'As the non-striker, you don't look at the umpire, you just wait for the roar as his finger goes up. The South Africans are jubilantly running into a huddle and suddenly they realise that it's not out...'

more difficult when the bowling is from round the wicket. So Donald changed to round the wicket.

Everything was going fine until Athers gloved it. A very faint glove. But when the bowler is coming round the wicket, his follow-through sometimes makes it quite difficult for the umpire to see the angle. I was standing wider than Steve Dunne and, let's put it this way, if I was the umpire I would have given it out.

So Atherton gloved it and Mark Boucher caught it. As the non-striker, you don't look at the umpire, you just wait for the roar as his finger goes up. The South Africans are jubilantly running into a huddle and suddenly they realise

it's not out. As I heard the roar die down, I knew that Atherton had escaped – and that Donald would be really steaming.

For a long time there had been questions asked about him: "Great fast bowler, but has he got a heart?" One thing we discovered during that series was that he certainly has got a lot of heart. In the previous match at Old Trafford, when he was trying to get Gus Fraser out, he ran in for hours bowling extremely quickly.

He had had battles with England before, notably against Atherton, and he was determined to win this one. At the end of the over I went up to Atherton and said: "You hit that, didn't you?" He gave a bit of a smile and replied: "I don't

'Atherton is the most stubborn batsman in cricket. He actually enjoys knowing that Donald is about to give him a barrage.'

'AD was furious with Boucher – but still patted him on the back.' Here Donald congratulates Boucher on catching Gough in the first innings

know." I was amused by it. I didn't think, "Oh God, we didn't need that." I thought: "Brilliant, this is going to be exciting here now." We both knew what was going to come up. The next hour was going to be exhilarating and full-on.

Michael Atherton was the worst person for Donald to have at the crease. He is the most stubborn batsman in cricket and in the same way that Steve Waugh loves proving people wrong, Atherton actually enjoys knowing that Donald is about to give him a barrage. I don't know if it was in his schooling or upbringing, whether he was just the little kid that everyone liked to have a go at, but he is a stubborn little man and he would have said: "Right, keep having a go at me. I did it in Johannesburg and I'll do it here. I will win us this game."

I think it helped him that it was South Africa, because he's got a good record against them. They fear him. They

view him as the one wicket they want and that's why it caused the reaction it did.

And then, in Donald's next over, that was exacerbated. Donald comes in to me, I play a wide one, nick it, it's just a regulation edge and I'm almost walking off and I don't look back. But I realise that Boucher must have dropped it because Donald is right in my face, just screaming. Not saying anything. Just screaming this howl of rage. I thought: "That's not your normal celebration, someone's messed up back there" – which was quite funny, because when Atherton nicked it, Boucher and Cullinan were two of the people who had had the odd word to say to Athers on the way past. So when Boucher dropped me, as he walked past I said: "A little bit quieter now, aren't you, Mark? Better concentrate on your keeping."

AD was furious with Boucher – but I noticed that at the

NASSER HUSSAIN'S ANALYSIS

'Donald is right in my face, just screaming. Not saying anything. Just screaming this howl of rage. I thought: "That's not your normal celebration…"'

end of the over, before going back to fine leg, he ran up and gave him a pat on the back and said, "Keep going," which shows what a team man he is.

That then got them even more angry. I've faced quicker bowling on pitches where you would expect it, like Jamaica, on the flying wicket where the game was abandoned earlier in 1998. But this was a benign pitch with an old ball and he gave us one of the most torrid sessions of bowling I've ever

experienced. We actually got a few more runs that evening because the bowling was full-on with plenty of bouncers and that gives you opportunities to score.

The next day I went on to get 50, then Stewart came in and played a nice innings when the pressure was off. We needed 60 to win and even we weren't going to collapse on this flat Trent Bridge wicket. But that hour was why we won the match and they didn't. Up until then, it was looking like a

More anguish for Allan Donald as, in the over after the Atherton incident, wicketkeeper Mark Boucher drops Nasser Hussain

NASSER HUSSAIN'S ANALYSIS

'If you look at the close-ups of that confrontation you can see in both people's eyes how important it was.'

Pistols at 22 yards: Michael Atherton and Allan Donald

typical English summer where we start all right, end up all right, but in between play dreadfully and lose the series. So the games at Old Trafford and Trent Bridge ended that trend.

But as I said to the boys when we toured South Africa in 1999/2000, they are vulnerable under pessure, and the more you hang in against them and put the onus on them to win the game, the more chance you've got. If you go two-nil down, they will tread all over you. You've got to stay with them and if you get to a close situation with them you've got a chance. That's why Old Trafford was the real key game of that 1998 series, because if we had gone two-nil down we would have been out of it.

Australia have accused South Africa of bottling it under pressure, but I just think that they are the norm – like any side, they can crack – whereas Australia, who handle pressure very well, are the exception.

We'll never know what would have happened if Dunne had given Atherton out or if Boucher had caught me. England have actually chased a fourth-innings target fairly well in recent years – if you asked us to bat first and get 250 or chase on the last day and get 250, we would take the chase. So I would have been pretty disappointed in our side if we had gone on to lose ... but with the England batting, you never know!

To this day I honestly don't know exactly what Donald said to Atherton. Some of it was in Afrikaans. I've seen highlights of it, because we have build-you-up videos and that is obviously one of them, so we use it occasionally and have a laugh at AD mouthing things to Ath. Usually, in a confrontation like that, Atherton just puts on that stare-to-scare-the-bowler-to-death ... not! This time, for a change, he actually spoke. But I think it was just something like, "Come

'At the end of the over I went up to Atherton and said: "You hit that, didn't you?" He gave a bit of a smile and replied: "I don't know".'

on then." It wasn't anything deep and philosophical. I'm not even sure if there was a sentence formulated there at all.

But if you look at the close-ups of that confrontation you can see in both people's eyes how important it was. It may appear to be a look of hatred, but Atherton and Donald are actually good mates. They have a mutual respect. You will often see Atherton drinking with Donald and Gary Kirsten, and in fact after that game AD and Kirsten came into our dressing room with a beer and sat with Atherton, Stewart and me for about an hour.

I can assure you the conversation was a bit more polite than what went on the previous afternoon!

Atherton and Hussain take a breather. The next day, England supporters gleefully swarmed on to the outfield after a pulsating victory

MIKE GATTING
V
SHAKOOR RANA

THE PROTAGONISTS

Mike Gatting
(Middlesex & England)
Aged 30. Playing his
60th Test and his 17th
as captain. Had led
England to an
impressive retaining of
the Ashes in Australia at
the start of the year.

Shakoor Rana
(Punjab & Railways)
Aged 51. In his 13th
season as a Test Match
umpire, after a career as
a useful all-rounder
from a cricketing family
(two brothers played
for Pakistan).

MIKE GATTING

SHAKOOR RANA

The umpire strikes back

Second Test · Faisalabad · December 8, 1987

*No one ever said playing Pakistan was easy. Touring teams have often complained
about the umpires, while the cricket and conditions are among the toughest in the world.
So when two such proud, stubborn men as Shakoor Rana and Mike Gatting
took the field together, it was bound to end in tears*

Few umpires' names provoke instant recognition like Shakoor Rana's. For a few days the former railway-man's confrontation with the England captain in a dusty manufacturing town in the Punjab made the front pages of newspapers all over the cricket-playing world and beyond. England had returned to Pakistan in November 1987 after reaching the World Cup Final, which they lost to Australia in Delhi. Pakistan had beaten England twice in the run-up to that, but now lost all three one-day internationals preceding the three Tests, by ever-greater margins.

After the third, the Pakistan team were bundled into two small buses to be driven from Peshawar to an audience

'YOU AND ME. OUTSIDE. NOW!'

'The whole incident, so far as I'm concerned, goes down as experience, and not an experience that I'd care to repeat, or that I'd like any other England cricketer to have to suffer, either.'

MIKE GATTING
IN HIS AUTOBIOGRAPHY,
'LEADING FROM THE
FRONT'

'Fingers were pointed and a heated argument, much embellished with unparliamentary language, broke out...'

England's bad boys: Chris Broad refusing to walk when given out at Lahore, and his captain being pulled away from umpire Shakoor Rana by short leg Bill Athey

'It was strictly a one-off thing in which we were, in my opinion, set up.'

MIKE GATTING
IN HIS AUTOBIOGRAPHY,
'LEADING FROM THE
FRONT'

with their country's president, General Zia, in Islamabad. This state of affairs must not be allowed to recur in the Tests.

The First Test was begun three days later in Lahore, where England found an underprepared pitch lying ready for the demon leg spinner, Abdul Qadir. He duly obliged with nine wickets in the first innings and four in the second – not, claimed the England management and captain, without quite a bit of assistance from the umpires.

That state of mind produced some undignified scenes, such as an England batsman refusing to walk off when given out and a late-night statement by the team manager at the England press's hotel in mid-Test. Pakistan won by

an innings and 87 runs early on the fourth afternoon.

The pitch for the Second Test in Faisalabad looked dry and dusty, too, the day before the match. But then came news from Lahore that Abdul Qadir's fitness was in doubt. He played in the end, but by that time the pitch had had a good watering and, after Mike Gatting won the toss, Chris Broad – the man who had refused to walk – scored a defiant century. His pugnacious captain made 79, but on the second morning, with the pitch dusting again, Qadir and the off spinner Iqbal Qasim took the last six wickets for 38 runs.

England's 292 began to look rather more healthy, however, half an hour after tea, when John Emburey took

Earlier in the innings, Shakoor Rana lectures Bruce French, Athey and Gatting after turning down a catch off Ijaz Ahmed (left)

Earlier in the innings, Shakoor Rana lectures Bruce French, Athey and Gatting after turning down a catch off Ijaz Ahmed (left)

'I am not surprised that the whole of Pakistan is proud of Shakoor. In the history of Pakistan cricket, he will rank along with Hanif, Zaheer, Imran and others for his "contributions" to Pakistan cricket.'

SUNIL GAVASKAR, 1988

two wickets in an over to have the home side reeling at 77 for 5. With three spinners in their side – off spinners Emburey and Eddie Hemmings, and slow left-armer Nick Cook – England were now eager to ram home their advantage. Only Salim Malik of the front-line batsmen remained and he had been joined by a Test debutant, Aamer Malik.

England's earlier frustration with the odd decision – notably when a close catch off Ijaz was turned down – had almost been forgotten. The visitors were now on top, yet the breakthrough just did not come.

As the close of play approached, they were striving to get through a Hemmings over quickly to give them a chance to get one more in before the end. Salim was on strike, and Gatting was keen to keep him there so that the last over could be bowled to Aamer. As Hemmings was coming in to bowl, Gatting waved David Capel up from deep square leg to a run-saving position. Shakoor Rana, the square-leg umpire, interpreted this as moving a fielder behind the batsman's back, and intervened with a shout of "Stop!" The other umpire, Khizar Hayat, not knowing what the fuss was about, called 'dead ball' as it was in flight.

Gatting snapped, the frustrations of the tour boiling over. Fingers were pointed and a heated argument, much embellished with unparliamentary language, broke out, as Gatting made it clear to Shakoor that he felt he had exceeded his authority. The umpire responded by calling Gatting a "f***ing cheating ****'. The row had the effect of ensuring that that was the final over and the day ended at 106 for 5.

Criticism on television of some of the previous day's umpiring decisions had led to the withdrawal of TV monitors from the press box. The light was beginning to go and the incident was at the far end of the pitch, all of which

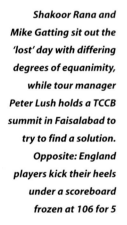

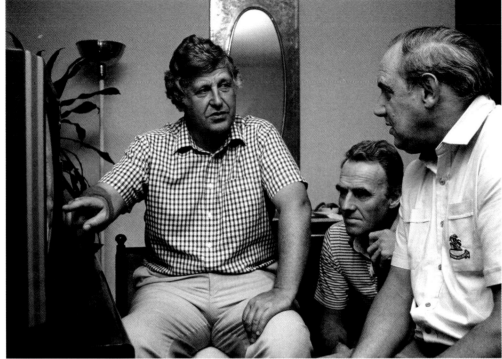

'We don't know anything about the two guys appointed, but we believe they will be better than having two Pakistani umpires.'

NEW ZEALAND CAPTAIN MARTIN CROWE APPROVING THE DECISION TO APPOINT NEUTRAL UMPIRES FOR THE 1990 SERIES. THE PAKISTANI BOARD WERE SO OFFENDED THAT THEY REVERSED THE DECISION. PAKISTAN WON 3-0.

Shakoor Rana and Mike Gatting sit out the 'lost' day with differing degrees of equanimity, while tour manager Peter Lush holds a TCCB summit in Faisalabad to try to find a solution. Opposite: England players kick their heels under a scoreboard frozen at 106 for 5

left the media in some confusion as to what had been going on. However, once back at the Serena Hotel, every correspondent found his phone buzzing. Television news close-ups of the confrontation were appearing in Britain and every sports editor wanted the inside story on what it was about.

After much late-night media hustle, the teams were again assembled at the Iqbal Stadium the following morning. Behind closed doors, discussions were going on and onlookers could gather that something might be amiss from the total inactivity of the groundstaff leaning on the roller in the middle as play was due to begin. The arguments raged all day, with Shakoor Rana demanding a full apology for the intemperate language used, Mike Gatting refusing to climb down and the whole situation being kept bubbling by unhelpful interventions from other parties.

There was no play on the third day of that Test and late in the day the England tour manager, Peter Lush, left by

Dear Shakoor Rana
I apologise for the bad language used during the 2nd day of the Test Match at Fisalabad (sic).
Mike Gatting

THE ENGLAND CAPTAIN'S
RELUCTANT APOLOGY

car for Lahore to see the President of the Pakistan Cricket Board, who, strangely, was out to dinner when he arrived and not available until the next day. That was a rest day. Around the hotel housing the teams, officials and the press, the speculation raged about how a way would be found to get out of the situation. Rhetoric was more in evidence than practicality.

On the fourth morning the England camp received an order from Lord's that the captain should make an unconditional apology, in writing – as the umpire was demanding. And so, half an hour late, play restarted, with Shakoor Rana having proudly pocketed a scrap of paper with that brief apology scrawled upon it.

Suggestions were made that an extra day might be added to the Test. We shall see, said Haseeb Ahsan, the Pakistan manager. But, after Pakistan had been dismissed 101 runs behind England, he revealed that no fewer than five of the Pakistan team (to their own evident surprise) were due to

Pakistan v England

Iqbal Stadium, Faisalabad, Pakistan   7.12.1987 - 12.12.1987
England won the toss and batted   Match Drawn

England	1st innings		2nd innings	
G.A.Gooch	c Aamer Malik b Iqbal Qasim ...	28	lbw b Abdul Qadir	65
B.C.Broad	b Tauseef Ahmed	116	st. Ashraf Ali b Abdul Qadir	14
C.W.J.Athey	c Aamer Malik b Abdul Qadir ...	27	b Mudassar Nazar	20
*M.W.Gatting	b Abdul Qadir	79	c Abdul Qadir b Iqbal Qasim	8
R.T.Robinson	c Ashraf Ali b Abdul Qadir	2	(8) not out	7
N.G.B.Cook	c Ashraf Ali b Iqbal Qasim	2		
D.J.Capel	c Aamer Malik b Abdul Qadir ...	1	lbw b Iqbal Qasim	2
J.E.Emburey	st. Ashraf Ali b Iqbal Qasim	15	(5) not out	10
N.A.Foster	c Aamer Malik b Iqbal Qasim ...	0	(6) c Javed Miandad b Abdul Qadir	0
+B.N.French	st. Ashraf Ali b Iqbal Qasim	2		
E.E.Hemmings	not out	1		
Extras	(b-10, lb-5, w-1, nb-3)	19	(b-1, lb-9, w-0, nb-1)	11
TOTAL	(all out) **292**		(for 6 wickets decl) **137**	

Fall of Wickets   1-73   2-124   3-241   4-249   5-258   1-47   2-102   3-107   4-115   5-115
                    6-259   7-288   8-288   9-288 10-292   6-120

Bowling Analysis	O	M	R	W		O	M	R	W
Aamer Malik	5	0	19	0		3	0	20	0
Mudassar Nazar	3	0	8	0		12	1	33	1
Abdul Qadir	42	7	105	4		15	3	45	3
Tauseef Ahmed	28	9	62	1					
Iqbal Qasim	35.2	7	83	5		10	2	29	2
Shoaib Mohammad	1	1	0	0					

Pakistan	1st innings		2nd innings	
Mudassar Nazar	c French b Foster	1	b Cook	4
Rameez Raja	c Gooch b Foster	12	not out	13
Salim Malik	b Cook	60	not out	28
*Javed Miandad	b Emburey	19		
Ijaz Ahmed	c Robinson b Emburey	11		
Shoaib Mohammad	b Emburey	0		
Aamer Malik	c French b Foster	5		
+Ashraf Ali	c French b Foster	4		
Abdul Qadir	c Gooch b Cook	38		
Iqbal Qasim	lbw b Hemmings	24		
Tauseef Ahmed	not out	5		
Extras	(b-0, lb-5, w-0, nb-7)	12	(b-4, lb-1, w-0, nb-1)	6
TOTAL	(all out) **191**		(for 1 wicket) **51**	

Fall of Wickets   1-11   2-22   3-58   4-77   5-77   1-15
                    6-115   7-122   8-123   9-175 10-191

Bowling Analysis	O	M	R	W		O	M	R	W
N.A.Foster	18	4	42	4		3	0	4	0
D.J.Capel	7	1	23	0					
E.E.Hemmings	18	5	35	1		7	3	16	0
J.E.Emburey	21	8	49	3		2	0	3	0
N.G.B.Cook	20.3	10	37	2		9	3	15	1
G.A.Gooch	2	1	4	0					
B.C.Broad	1	0	4	0					

Umpires: Khizar Hayat, Shakoor Rana   **Man of the Match:** B.C.Broad

get married between this Test and the next, which would make it impossible. The Test petered out in a draw.

Senior figures from the Test and County Cricket Board arrived before the Third Test and, after hearing the players' version of events, awarded them each a £1,000 'hardship bonus'. Despite this undiplomatic gesture, the final Test was played as a good, straight contest, with good umpiring – and drawn. But well over a decade would go by before England would return to play another Test in Pakistan.

NASSER HUSSAIN'S ANALYSIS

'You can see how it would get out of hand – they're both very proud people'

'Pakistan is not the easiest of tours by anyone's standards. Playing cricket there really is hard work.'

The only way a cricket captain can get into the situation that Mike Gatting did here is because there is so much stress and tension weighing on him. It's not the sort of thing he does on the first morning of the First Test of the season. England had recently lost the World Cup Final, and no doubt the whole winter had been geared towards the World Cup. That was the Final in which Gatting got out by playing the reverse sweep, so that little disaster would have been weighing heavily on his mind.

Every night on tour, when you go back to your hotel room, you ask yourself what sort of winter you're having, both personally and as a team. Having gone to the subcontinent, reached the World Cup Final and then won the one-day series, he has actually had a very good winter – but what everyone will remember is the reverse sweep. That one shot has spoilt his year. So now he is trying to drag back the winter and finish it on a high note.

The trouble is, he's trying to do it in Pakistan, which is not the easiest of tours by anyone's standards. Playing cricket there really is hard work, especially when Pakistan have a strong side, as they did then. On top of all that there was pressure

on the Pakistanis themselves because they had had a poor World Cup. Things were so bad that their Prime Minister had called them in for a chat. Cricket is huge in Pakistan: they will do almost anything not to lose a Test match, and it often seems to rub the opposition up the wrong way.

Then a few things happen in the First Test that make the England team feel everything is stacked against them. They probably get into a bit of a siege mentality. You can imagine all the pressures building up during a long, hard winter away.

When you're counting down the days until the end of the tour, the captain doesn't have the reserves of patience that he might have had when he set out. At the beginning of the 1999/2000 tour to South Africa and Zimbabwe, I would have let a lot of things pass, such as a fielder throwing the ball in 10 yards over the keeper's head. But by the end of the tour, I'd be having a double teapot out in the middle of the pitch and effing and blinding at him. What with the constant pressures of the media, after four months of it you're a little bit closer to boiling point and it doesn't take much to push you over the top. And that's obviously how Mike Gatting was feeling by the time the team arrived in Faisalabad.

NASSER HUSSAIN'S ANALYSIS

'When you're touring, you want to go into your dressing room with some kind of positive, especially somewhere like Pakistan – it makes the evenings go quicker.'

So now they've got Pakistan at 77 for 5 and for the England captain it's a case of seizing the moment. It's a low-scoring game and you know that every run is vital, particularly on a wearing Pakistan pitch where you're going to have Abdul Qadir and Iqbal Qasim bowling at you in the second innings. But if you get a couple of wickets, that's it, you've bowled them out.

When you're touring, you want to go into your dressing room with some kind of positive, especially somewhere like Pakistan – it makes the evenings go quicker. So Gatting is desperately trying to get that one last wicket so he can say he's had a good day. He also wants to get another over in, and he wants to keep Salim Malik on strike so they can bowl that last over at the new boy.

Eddie Hemmings is bustling through his over. Suddenly Gatt remembers that he wanted to bring up the deep square leg, because otherwise the batsman just has to flick the off-spinner off his pads and he's away down to the other end. He doesn't want to stop Eddie in his run-up because that will waste time, so he just quietly waves the fielder up. I've done it often enough for Essex, and even for England,

and then you think: "Hold on, this is how the Gatt incident started!" You're not trying to cheat or be unfair, you've just forgotten something very important.

Rightfully, the square-leg umpire has pulled him up on it – and suddenly everything has come to a head.

You can see how it would get out of hand, especially with Gatt and a Pakistani umpire. They are both very proud people. A Pakistani umpire is not going to stand down in Pakistan, that is for certain. He knows his country is going to back him because they are such a proud people. Gatt's not going to stand down either, so it gets a bit heated.

Gatting had been a successful captain. Phillip DeFreitas has often told me that Gatt was a good skipper – "one of us". Knowing that his team believed in him and were right behind him, Gatting probably thought he should make a stand and say: "Enough's enough." But as captain, once there are pictures of you wagging your finger at the umpire and being pulled away by your teammates, you're obviously in big trouble.

The next day, Lord's and the then TCCB would have been flapping because this is exactly the kind of thing they hate: having to make a choice between their own players and the

Above: Mike Gatting checks the Faisalabad pitch before the match. Opposite: Shakoor Rana with local admirers

NASSER HUSSAIN'S ANALYSIS

'Phillip DeFreitas
has often told me
that Gatt was a
good skipper –
"one of us".
Knowing that his
team believed in
him and were
right behind him,
Gatting probably
thought he should
make a stand...'

Mike Gatting – a cricketer's cricketer – finds a haven in the Faisalabad dressing room while the Pakistan flag hangs over an empty pitch

governing body of a fellow Test-playing nation. They would have had frantic meeetings about it.

As luck would have it, the next tour after that was an England A Team tour in 1995/96 which I captained, and I was dragged in to Lord's beforehand to be reminded that it was a bridge-building tour. We quite enjoyed it, to be honest. The hotels and the welcome we received were excellent. Pakistan has great places to visit, but whereas in Australia,

once you leave the cricket ground, everything's easy – the taxis, the hotels, the food – Pakistan is a tough tour in a hot country where you have to be careful about what you eat.

It's amazing to think that England's trip to Pakistan in 2000/2001 will be the first senior tour there since that Mike Gatting visit back in 1987. Our return is long overdue, and this time I hope that everyone will enjoy it. But there's one thing we all know: the cricket will still be very hard indeed.

NASSER HUSSAIN'S ANALYSIS

'Lord's and the then TCCB would have been flapping because this is exactly the kind of thing they hate: having to make a choice between their own players and the governing body of a fellow Test-playing nation.'

Culture clash on a cricket-free Friday... Behind the pavilion, Shakoor Rana leads a group including Pakistan players in prayer. Out on the pitch, England wonder if play will ever start

Trench warfare

MAY & COWDREY V RAMADHIN · EDGBASTON · 1957

RHODES & HIRST V AUSTRALIA · THE OVAL · 1902

ATHERTON V SOUTH AFRICA · JOHANNESBURG · 1995

BAILEY & WATSON V AUSTRALIA · LORD'S · 1953

HOBBS & SUTCLIFFE V AUSTRALIA · MELBOURNE · 1928/9

Opposite: Jack Russell encourages Michael Atherton in his long vigil at Johannesburg
This page: Peter May, Hugh Trumble, Mike Atherton, a batless Keith Miller, and Jack Hobbs & Herbert Sutcliffe

PETER MAY & COLIN COWDREY
V
SONNY RAMADHIN

PETER MAY

COLIN COWDREY

SONNY RAMADHIN

The riddle of Ramadhin

First Test · Edgbaston · June 1-4, 1957

West Indian spin magician Sonny Ramadhin tied the English batsmen in such knots that
they decided there was only one solution: blast their way out of trouble. Not a good idea.
Now they were 288 behind on the first innings, and still no nearer to solving the puzzle…

When England batsmen of modern times may have shivered at the thought of trying to deal with the devilment of Shane Warne, they are by no means unique. In the Fifties the West Indies had their own version – Sonny Ramadhin. The little Trinidadian's mixture of leg- and off-breaks, allied to the left-arm spin of Alf Valentine, had brought his team their first ever Test victory in England seven years before at Lord's, when the calypso had celebrated them as *"those two pals of mine"*. Ramadhin had taken 26 wickets in the four Tests of that 1950 series and Valentine 33, and the West Indies had stunned their hosts by winning 3-1. Now they

'Out in the middle
Sonny Ramadhin's
fingers grew more
and more tired as
he spun over after
over – a record 129
of them in all...'

E.W. SWANTON
IN 'FROM ARLOTT TO
AGGERS: 40 YEARS OF
TEST MATCH SPECIAL'.
THIS WAS THE FIRST EVER
'TEST MATCH SPECIAL'

were back in England in support of a formidable batting side. But England were also formidable, and had the belief that they now knew how to play the two spinners.

Perhaps because this Test started in May, the West Indies left Valentine out. Young Gary Sobers could bowl slow left arm, but he was not needed on the first day as England discovered that they had not, after all, broken the Ramadhin hoodoo. They were all out by tea for 186.

They had tried to put Ramadhin to the sword and had perished. The little man had taken seven for 49 and proved

he could still run rings round them. Bowling with sleeves rolled down, making detection of his wrist action difficult, and a fast arm action, he had bowled four of his victims, achieving his success more through apprehension than excessive turn. He had operated in harness with a new fast bowler, Roy Gilchrist, who looked distinctly nippy. The prospect of a difficult series stretched ahead of England.

By the close of the first day that was underlined, with the West Indies 83 for 1 thanks to Clyde Walcott and the debutant Rohan Kanhai. The West Indies lost only four

*Sonny Ramadhin
bowls to Peter May –
one of the record
1,374 balls bowled
by the Trinidadian
in the match*

Right: Peter May acknowledges the applause for his 200. By the time he declared he was 285 not out

wickets the next day and, at 316 for 5, were now 130 ahead. Walcott had made 90, Everton Weekes at least had been bowled by Fred Trueman for only 9, but the third 'W', Frank Worrell, was well set on 48 and with him the burgeoning batting talent of 'Collie' Smith. Smith carried on next day to make 161 after Worrell had been bowled by Brian Statham for 81.

The West Indies were finally all out for 474, a lead of 288. With two-and-a-half days to go, England were not optimistic. The captain, Peter May, talked to the batsmen about how they were going to tackle the problem of Ramadhin, suggesting that perhaps the first-innings impetuosity was not the answer. His words seemed to be bearing fruit, as an opening stand of 63 by Peter Richardson and Brian Close gave notice of defiance. But then Ramadhin broke through, first having Richardson caught close to the wicket for 34 and in his next over bowling Doug Insole for a duck.

At 65 for 2, Peter May walked in to bat, glancing at the pantile-roofed scoreboard showing him that England still needed another 223 runs to avoid an innings defeat. Still trying in vain to pick Ramadhin's variations, May trusted himself early on to go for a cover drive as soon as he overpitched and felt much better as he watched the ball speed to the boundary. The day ended with May and Close having added 37 at 102 for 2 and two more days lying dauntingly ahead after the rest day.

May had convinced himself over the weekend that his side were quite capable of saving this Test. The dream was shattered after twenty minutes on Monday morning when Gilchrist had Close caught at slip for 42.

At 113 for 3, England were 175 behind as Colin Cowdrey walked out to join his old friend Peter May.

Gilchrist had got the wicket, but they knew that their problems would come from Ramadhin, and had spent much of the weekend discussing him. They had agreed that they must play him as an off-spinner and just hope they missed the sharp away turn of the undetected leg-break.

Soon after Cowdrey had joined him, May berated himself for playing a loose shot past mid on and asked his partner to tick him off if he saw him doing that again. Cowdrey cut out aggressive shots almost entirely and started using his pads to Ramadhin. As the LBW law then stood, he was safe to do so to any ball pitching outside the off stump, though the little Trinidadian was to give voice to many appeals and years afterwards to continue to harbour the belief that at least one of them must have been justified. The next man in, Trevor Bailey, was constantly reaching for his gloves as the sound of each shout penetrated the dressing room. But on they went.

The batsmen constantly played forward to Ramadhin, keeping their concentration with frequent mid-pitch discussions. Defence was the prime consideration, but May, particularly, turned down no opportunity to score. After four hours and ten minutes he reached his hundred and soon after tea they ensured that the West Indies would have to bat again. Going into the innings without the medium pace of Worrell, who had a leg injury, late in the day the West Indies also lost Gilchrist, so the main foil to Ramadhin was now Denis Atkinson, with his off breaks. Sobers and Smith, too, had plenty of the bowling burden to shoulder.

England lost only one wicket on that fourth day. At the close they were 90 runs ahead at 378 for 3 with May already closing on his double century at 193 and Cowdrey 78. Watching his determined, elegant friend, Cowdrey reckoned he had never witnessed a finer innings. They had already batted for nearly five-and-three-quarter hours together and added 265. Sonny Ramadhin had bowled 48 overs that day, 20 of them maidens, and although he had gone wicketless had conceded only 74 runs.

But the final day began with England still far from safe. May reached the only double hundred of his career and just before lunch Cowdrey, too, got to three figures. Scoring started to become easier, and a steer from Cowdrey down to third man brought the partnership to 400. That was followed by May advancing down the pitch to hit Sobers high into the pavilion for six to take him to 250.

When Cowdrey had reached 154, he lofted Collie Smith to long-on, where he was caught on the boundary. England were 524 for 4. The fourth wicket had added 411 and taken them from a position of real peril to the prosperity of being 236 ahead. It remains the record fourth-wicket stand in all Test cricket and England's highest for any wicket.

Mentally and physically exhausted, Peter May started to consider the possibility of a declaration. Then he remembered the power of the three 'Ws', Smith, Sobers and the new man, Kanhai, and that the West Indies themselves had only managed to take two wickets in nine hours' play.

Trevor Bailey, after waiting with his pads on for four sessions of play, had been relieved of that position and the new batsman was Godfrey Evans.

May knew they had saved the match. Now, he did not want to throw that away on a rash declaration. When he did declare at 583 for 4, leaving the West Indies two hours and twenty minutes to bat, he had been in for nearly ten hours and had scored 285 priceless runs.

In the light of what subsequently happened, perhaps May might have declared earlier. Fred Trueman quickly removed both openers and then the Surrey spinners, Jim Laker and Tony Lock, reduced the West Indies to 72 for 7 when the umpires called time. Maybe a few more overs would have brought England an extraordinary win, though May did not believe so. What he and Cowdrey had done, though, was to ensure that Ramadhin was no longer a threat in the series. England won the Second, Fourth and Fifth Tests, each by an innings.

The two England batting heroes would go on to knighthoods and each to the presidency of MCC. Sonny Ramadhin would retire to run a pub in a small moorland town near Manchester.

England v West Indies

Edgbaston, Birmingham, England
England won the toss and batted

30.5.1957 - 4.6.1957
Match Drawn

England	1st innings		2nd innings	
P.E.Richardson	c Walcott b Ramadhin	47	c sub b Ramadhin	34
D.B.Close	c Kanhai b Gilchrist	15	c Weekes b Gilchrist	42
D.J.Insole	b Ramadhin	20	b Ramadhin	0
*P.B.H.May	c Weekes b Ramadhin	30	not out	285
M.C.Cowdrey	c Gilchrist b Ramadhin	4	c subs b Smith	154
T.E.Bailey	b Ramadhin	1		
G.A.R.Lock	b Ramadhin	0		
+T.G.Evans	b Gilchrist	14	(6) not out	29
J.C.Lake	rb Ramadhin	7		
F.S.Trueman	not out	29		
J.B.Statham	b Atkinson	13		
Extras	(b-3, lb-3, w-0, nb-0)	6	(b-23, lb-16, w-0, nb-0)	39
TOTAL	(all out)	186	(for 4 wickets declared)	583

Fall of Wickets	1-32	2-61	3-104	4-115	5-116	1-63	2-65	3-113	4-524
	6-118	7-121	8-130	9-150	10-186				

Bowling Analysis	O	M	R	W	O	M	R	W
F.M.M.Worrell	9	1	27	0				
R.Gilchrist	27	4	74	2	26	2	67	1
S.Ramadhin	31	16	49	7	98	35	179	2
D.StE.Atkinson	12.4	3	30	1	72	29	137	0
G.StA.Sobers					30	4	77	0
O.G.Smith					26	4	72	1
J.D.C.Goddard					6	2	12	0

West Indies	1st innings		2nd innings	
B.H.Pairaudeau	b Trueman	1	b Trueman	7
+R.B.Kanhai	LBW b Statham	42	c Close b Trueman	1
C.L.Walcott	c Evans b Laker	90	(6) c Lock b Laker	1
E.deC.Weekes	b Trueman	9	c Trueman b Lock	33
G.StA.Sobers	c Bailey b Statham	53	(3) c Cowdrey b Lock	14
O.G.Smith	LBW b Laker	161	(7) LBW b Laker	5
F.M.M.Worrell	b Statham	81	(5) c May b Lock	0
*J.D.C.Goddard	c Lock b Laker	24	not out	0
D.StE.Atkinson	c Statham b Laker	1	not out	4
S.Ramadhin	not out	5		
R.Gilchrist	run out	0		
Extras	(b-1, lb-6, w-0, nb-0)	7	(b-7, lb-0, w-0, nb-0)	7
TOTAL	(all out)	474	(for 7 wickets)	72

Fall of Wickets	1-4	2-83	3-120	4-183	5-197	1-1	2-9	3-25	4-27	5-43
	6-387	7-466	8-469	9-474	10-474	6-66	7-68			

Bowling Analysis	O	M	R	W	O	M	R	W
J.B.Statham	39	4	114	3	2	0	6	0
F.S.Trueman	30	4	99	2	5	3	7	2
T.E.Bailey	34	11	80	0				
J.C.Laker	54	17	119	4	24	20	13	2
G.A.R.Lock	34.4	15	55	0	27	19	31	3
D.B.Close					2	1	8	0

Umpires: D.E.Davies, C.S.Elliott

NASSER HUSSAIN'S ANALYSIS

'The cat-and-mouse battle between spinner and batsmen'

'The LBW rule was tough for Ramadhin, and I'm sure that under today's laws he would get a lot of wickets.'

To attack or not attack the spinner, that is the question. Normally you get after someone when they have the voodoo over you and you're trying to take away the impetus, which is obviously what England tried to do against Sonny Ramadhin in the first innings of this match. But then that didn't work, so Peter May and Colin Cowdrey evidently changed tactics to just sitting on him and milking him around. That's one way to survive, but to put on over 400 together doing that is amazing.

With Ramadhin's stock ball being the off break, the rule that you couldn't be out to a ball pitching outside off stump must have made it very difficult for him, because if he pitched a turning ball on the wicket, it would go down the leg side. If that rule applied today, people would sweep him all the time.

On the question of whether to attack or defend, I take the view that if it is turning in to the bat – an off spinner – I will use my feet to try and hit him. The more it's turning, the more positive I'll be. Essex have tended to prepare turning wickets at Chelmsford, Ilford, Colchester and Southend for John Childs, David Acfield, Ray East and Peter Such, so I learned to play off-spin early in my career. But when I reached Test level I found it was more difficult because the teams you play against mainly turn it away from the bat.

England have obviously had various discussions about spin over the past few years. In 1998/99 in Australia we took advice from Peter Philpott, the guru of Aussie spin. It didn't prove very successful, because we all got out to McGill and Warne! But it was interesting, especially for Mike Atherton and me, having both played for England Schools as leg spinners.

Philpott viewed Warne as someone you should attack, because he's at you all the time, attacking you, drifting it in, turning it away, and if you just sit there and let him bowl at you with three or four men round the bat, the pressure is all on you and it's only a matter of time before you make a mistake. Whereas McGill he viewed as someone that you should sit on because, even though he bowls some magical balls that turn even more than Warne, he does bowl the odd long hop or full toss that you can hit.

It worked for me with McGill but I was never very comfortable taking the attack to Warne. In fact, Sachin

NASSER HUSSAIN'S ANALYSIS

'When you first go in against spin it can be really difficult, and you begin to wonder where you're going to get a run from.'

Tendulkar is really the only batsman who has managed it, and that's why the Australians have such respect for him. To take Warne on, you have to be able to play the Gooch slog-sweep over square leg. When Tendulkar began hitting sixes with that shot against Warne, for once Warne was not in control.

When you first go in against spin, with men clustered round the bat appealing for everything, it can be really difficult, and you begin to wonder where you're going to get a run from. But once you reach 20 or 30, it becomes a bit easier – which is why a partnership like the one between May and Cowdrey is so crucial.

The tactical battle between a spinner and the batsmen is a real cat-and-mouse, not just on the day but also in the long term. When May and Cowdrey worked out that they could nullify the threat of Sonny Ramadhin by padding him away, you could say that he was 'found out'.

When we first saw Paul Adams, the South African left-arm spinner, our batsmen didn't have a clue. But after analysing him on videotape, we figured out how to play him by watching the ball in his hand. So then Adams had to change by trying to cover up his hand before he bowled.

I remember facing Malcolm Marshall in my early days and not knowing which way he was going to swing it until Graham Gooch told me: "Just watch the ball in his hand as he runs up." I said: "Great, I can just about see the ball, let alone which side the shiny side is on!" But then Marshall worked out that Gooch was watching his hand, so he began to run in with his hands together.

The in-swinging yorkers of Waqar Younis and Wasim Akram don't seem as potent as they used to be, partly because batsmen have worked out that if they watch the ball in their hands, they can see from the shine which way it will swing. The Pakistanis countered that by covering up the ball in their run-up.

So then batting sides came up with the theory that the non-striker should watch the bowler turn at his mark, to see which side he was putting the shine on, and hold his bat in a certain way to give a message to the receiving batsman. I never liked that because it just takes one dopy partner to be leaning on his bat forgetting to give you the message – and meanwhile you're peering at his bat wondering: "Is that an inswinger or an outswinger?"

The way that May and Cowdrey worked out how to play Ramadhin and Alf Valentine was based on a technicality that the LBW law at the time enabled them to do. It was a tough rule for Ramadhin, and I'm sure that under today's laws he would get a lot of wickets.

I note that Trevor Bailey spent 24 hours with his pads on waiting for either May or Cowdrey to get out. Well, I can sympathise there, Trevor. I used to bat after Gooch and Mark Waugh at Essex, and I can tell you, it took a lot of patience!

Sonny Ramadhin shows Don Bradman how he does it

GEORGE HIRST & WILFRED RHODES
V
HUGH TRUMBLE

THE PROTAGONISTS

George Hirst
(Yorkshire & England)
Aged 30. Playing his ninth Test, having made 269 runs before it. He would finish with 790 runs and 59 wickets from his 24 Tests.

Wilfred Rhodes
(Yorkshire and England)
Aged 24. Playing his eighth Test. He had so far batted only at 10 or 11, but during his 58 Tests he would also open the batting, make two centuries and finish with 2,325 runs as well as his 127 wickets. (In first-class cricket he took a world record 4,187 wickets, passing 100 wickets in 23 seasons.)

Hugh Trumble
(Victoria & Australia)
Aged 35. Playing his 27th Test, having taken 117 of his eventual 141 wickets. He captained Australia twice and became secretary of the Melbourne Cricket Club.

WILFRED RHODES

HUGH TRUMBLE

GEORGE HIRST

'We'll get 'em in singles'

Fifth Test • The Oval • August 13, 1902

England's first home win of the Twentieth Century stretched their supporters' nerves to breaking point. It was illuminated by the most explosive Test innings ever by an Englishman – but Gilbert Jessop's derring-do would have done no good had it not been for the nerveless defiance of two gritty Yorkshiremen

We'll get 'em in singles. A phrase that has passed into cricket folklore has made this partnership famous. It did not win the Ashes; they had already been retained in a wet summer by Australia in an incredible match at Old Trafford a fortnight before, when they won by three runs to go 2-0 up with one match remaining. But this phlegmatic partnership withstood unbearable tension to win a historic game for England, and give just reward to one of cricket's great individual innings.

It featured two legendary Yorkshiremen: George Hirst and Wilfred Rhodes. Hirst was a 31-year-old left-arm fast-medium bowler and useful batsman, particularly strong on

'Wilfred Rhodes is
Yorkshire's latest,
and, it may be,
greatest discovery.'

W.G. GRACE
'W.G. – CRICKETING
REMINISCENCES
AND PERSONAL
RECOLLECTIONS'

Yorkshire heroes
of a century ago
– the legendary
Wilfred Rhodes (far
left) and George Hirst

*Let's go to work…
Gilbert Jessop, who
thumped 104 to set up
England's last-gasp win;
Bill Lockwood, who took
five for 45 in Australia's
second innings; and
Hugh Trumble, who
somehow finished on
the losing side despite
bowling unchanged
throughout two innings,
taking 12 wickets, and
scoring 71 runs without
being dismissed*

*'No one has ever
driven the ball
so hard, so high
and so often in so
many different
directions.'*

C. B. FRY
ON GILBERT JESSOP

the leg side. Rhodes was six years his junior, a slow left-arm bowler who would go on to take more first-class wickets than anyone else and who would bat in his career both first and last for England.

Test matches at that time were played over three days,

and this one might well, had things panned out differently, have become known as Trumble's match. Hugh Trumble came in to bat for Australia at 175 for 7 and was 64 not out when Australia were all out at the end of the first day (on which England had bowled 124 overs) for 324. Hirst

had taken 5 for 77. The second day belonged even more emphatically to Trumble – with the ball this time – on a damp pitch. The lanky purveyor of lively-paced off spin took the new ball and soon caused havoc in the England batting. The seventh wicket fell with 38 still needed to avoid the follow-on.

Hirst and Lockwood prevented that happening, before Hirst was caught and bowled for 43 by Trumble, who bowled unchanged for 31 overs, in which he took 8 for 65. Well before tea, England had been dismissed for 183. It is a testimony to Trumble's accuracy that four of his eight victims were bowled.

So, on the second afternoon, Australia started their second innings 141 runs ahead. With such a powerful

position, it is unlikely that alarm bells rang when first the great Victor Trumper was run out for 2 and then Bill Lockwood bowled Reggie Duff, the other opener, for 6 and Australia were 9 for 2. He had Joe Darling caught in the gully for 15, when the score had reached 31, but Clem Hill and Monty Noble put on 40 for the fourth wicket to take the lead past 200. Len Braund made the next breakthrough with the wickets of Noble and Syd Gregory, and with Hirst removing Hill for 34, Lockwood getting another and Rhodes removing Jack Saunders just before the close of play, Australia were 114 for 8 at the end of the second day, 255 ahead and not entirely clear of danger.

There was a heavy dew that night on the uncovered

The Australian tourists of 1902, posing proudly for the photographer, were portrayed in a less flattering light by a cartoonist after a defeat by Yorkshire

A packed crowd at The Oval get ready to throw their boaters in the air. Below: Monty Noble was wicketless despite what the cartoonist called his 'curve of beauty', while the Hon F.S. Jackson played sheet anchor to Jessop's runaway train

pitch and Lockwood quickly finished off the Australian innings for the addition of only seven more runs. Lockwood had taken 5 for 45 and England, in a day's play less half an hour, would need 263 to win.

There was still life in the pitch for Trumble and Saunders to exploit and it was Saunders, bowling from the Vauxhall end, less naggingly accurate than Trumble, who started to cause mayhem. He bowled Archie MacLaren for 2, Johnny Tyldesley for a duck and Lionel Palairet for 6 and England were 10 for 3 and now extremely unlikely to reach their target. It was even less likely when he had had Tom Hayward caught behind for 7 and Trumble had done the same to Braund for 2. England were all but finished at 48 for 5.

The Honourable F. S. Jackson – Stanley Jackson – of Yorkshire was now joined by Gilbert Jessop from Gloucestershire, whose qualities as a batsman were not always universally appreciated at that time (even though he had scored 157 in an hour the previous year against the

West Indies!). By lunch they had taken the total to 87, not without some fortune, as Jessop survived a missed stumping and a dropped catch.

After the interval, Jessop, nicknamed 'The Croucher' for his rather stooped stance, started to take the attack to Australia with gusto, charging down the wicket to Trumble and Saunders, as Jackson played the sheet-anchor role admirably. Saunders particularly suffered, losing his length and being despatched for 17 in one over. Trumble, meanwhile, as he did in the first innings, was to bowl unchanged throughout the innings from the Pavilion End and it was he who finally managed to break the sixth-wicket partnership, having Jackson caught and bowled for 49, but not before he and Jessop had added 109 together.

There were 106 more runs needed as George Hirst came in to join Jessop. Almost immediately he survived a very confident appeal for LBW from Trumble. Jessop, though, was now attacking even that admirable bowler. In one over he twice hit him back over his head for six into the pavilion. His 100 came in only 75 minutes and, although it was his only Test century, it is still the second-fastest in history in terms of time. He had faced 76 balls.

Saunders was replaced by Warwick Armstrong with his leg spin, which proved to be more to the taste of Hirst than Jessop, who was frustrated by it. After finding himself shackled by it, he popped one up to short leg, where Noble took the catch and his historic innings had ended for 104, his contribution to the 139 runs scored while he was in. With Jessop gone, at 187 for 7 and 76 still needed, it seemed likely that England's chances had also vanished.

The lead role now passed to Hirst, as Lockwood came in to join him. Hirst seemed confident and dominated their eighth-wicket stand of 27, to which Lockwood contributed just two before Trumble had him LBW. The wicketkeeper, Dick Lilley, came in at 214 for 8 and contributed 16 of the ninth-wicket stand of 34, before Trumble had him caught at mid-off.

So near and yet so far. At 248 for 9, with 15 runs still needed, the last man, Wilfred Rhodes, was coming in to join George Hirst.

The legend that Hirst greeted Rhodes with, "We'll get 'em in singles" was actually created by the great cricket writer Neville Cardus, who was sometimes given, perhaps forgivably, to such flights of fancy. Years later, having been asked if those words had been said, Rhodes said: "Of course not! If we could have hit fours, we would have done."

But Hugh Trumble was a master bowler. He had already bowled throughout Australia's time in the field and had gathered 12 wickets. Now he could scent victory and was giving nothing away.

The two Yorkshiremen kept their patience. Refusing to chance their arm, they slowly chipped away at the target, single by single, amidst tension that was almost tangible in a packed Oval crowd. One shot for two broke the sequence of ones and dots. Finally, yet another single from Hirst brought the scores level. It was left to Rhodes to play Trumble away for the winning run to the accompaniment of bowler hats and boaters being hurled in the air as the crowd erupted in a relieved roar of celebration. Hirst was 58 not out, Rhodes 6, and England had won by one wicket.

England v Australia

The Oval, London, England
Australia won the toss and batted

11.8.1902 - 13.8.1902
England won by 1 wicket

Australia	1st innings		2nd innings	
V.T.Trumper	b Hirst	42	run out	2
R.A.Duff	c Lilley b Hirst	23	b Lockwood	6
C.Hill	b Hirst	11	c MacLaren b Hirst	34
*J.Darling	c Lilley b Hirst	3	c MacLaren b Lockwood	15
M.A.Noble	c & b Jackson	52	b Braund	13
S.E.Gregory	b Hirst	23	b Braund	9
W.W.Armstrong	b Jackson	17	b Lockwood	21
A.J.Y Hopkins	c MacLaren b Lockwood	40	c Lilley b Lockwood	3
H.Trumble	not out	64	(10) not out	7
+J.J.Kelly	c Rhodes b Braund	39	(11) lbw b Lockwood	0
J.V.Saunders	lbw b Braund	0	(9) c Tyldesley b Rhodes	2
Extras	(b-5, lb-3, w-0, nb-2)	10	(b-7, lb-2, w-0, nb-0)	9
TOTAL	(all out)	324	(all out)	121

Fall of Wickets	1-47	2-63	3-69	4-82	5-126	1-6	2-9	3-31	4-71	5-75
	6-174	7-175	8-256	9-324	10-324	6-91	7-99	8-114	9-115	10-121

Bowling Analysis	O	M	R	W		O	M	R	W
W.H.Lockwood	24	2	85	1		20	6	45	5
W.Rhodes	28	9	46	0		22	7	38	1
G.H.Hirst	29	5	77	5		5	1	7	1
L.C.Braund	16.5	5	29	2		9	1	15	2
Hon.F.S.Jackson	20	4	66	2		4	3	7	0
G.L.Jessop	6	2	11	0					

England	1st innings		2nd innings	
*A.C.MacLaren	c Armstrong b Trumble	10	b Saunders	2
L.C.H.Palairet	b Trumble	20	b Saunders	6
J.T.Tyldesley	b Trumble	33	b Saunders	0
T.W.Hayward	b Trumble	0	c Kelly b Saunders	7
Hon.F.S.Jackson	c Armstrong b Saunders	2	c & b Trumble	49
L.C.Braund	c Hill b Trumble	22	c Kelly b Trumble	2
G.L.Jessop	b Trumble	13	c Noble b Armstrong	104
G.H.Hirst	c & b Trumble	43	not out	58
W.H.Lockwood	c Noble b Saunders	25	lbw b Trumble	2
+A.F.A.Lilley	c Trumper b Trumble	0	c Darling b Trumble	16
W.Rhodes	not out	0	not out	6
Extras	(b-13, lb-2, w-0, nb-0)	15	(b-5, lb-6, w-0, nb-0)	11
TOTAL	(all out)	183	(for 9 wickets)	263

Fall of Wickets	1-31	2-36	3-62	4-67	5-67	1-5	2-5	3-10	4-31	5-48
	6-83	7-137	8-179	9-183	10-183	6-157	7-187	8-214	9-248	

Bowling Analysis	O	M	R	W		O	M	R	W
H.Trumble	31	13	65	8		33.5	4	108	4
J.V.Saunders	23	7	79	2		24	3	105	4
M.A.Noble	7	3	24	0		5	0	11	0
W.W.Armstrong	4	0	28	1					

Umpires: C.E.Richardson, A.A.White

NASSER HUSSAIN'S ANALYSIS

'There's something about the Yorkshire mentality...'

Tyke-casting... Gough comes from the same mould as Hirst (who's actually standing on a step) and Rhodes

If Rhodes and Hirst really did "get 'em in singles", it would have made dreadful viewing for their teammates, because when you're chasing a target, the one thing the guys in the dressing room want to see is boundaries. I know it sounds obvious, but nothing lifts a side more. We've been in so many tight games, such as the tied Test against Zimbabwe, and singles are no good because they just prolong the agony.

By the sound of it, George Hirst and Wilfred Rhodes were typical Yorkshiremen. There's something about the Yorkshire mentality that makes their cricketers want to be the hero in a tough situation. They all have that gritty leave-it-to-me attitude – and none more so than Darren Gough. At Centurion Park, in our 1999 Test against South Africa, Gough hit the winning runs with Chris

Silverwood at the other end. It was a situation made for him. Before he went in to bat, he was sitting next to me on the balcony saying: "Am I going to get in, am I going to get in?" I said: "Yes, you're going to need four and you're going to hit the boundary" – praying that that was not going to happen and that Stewart and Vaughan would see it through. But as soon as he got up, he said: "Leave it to me." And went and hit the winning boundary.

So often when we have won, Darren Gough has been right there in the middle of it all. At Headingley in 1998 he takes the last South African wicket and there he is with a stump in his hand. At Melbourne in 1998, he takes the last Australian wicket. And then he goes out and scores the winning runs at Centurion in 1999. But I don't think Goughie ever said: "We'll get 'em in singles."

NASSER HUSSAIN'S ANALYSIS

'So many times, when we have won, Darren Gough has been right there in the middle of it all.'

Darren Gough – a man who loves to be at the centre of the action

CRICKET'S GREATEST BATTLES

MICHAEL ATHERTON
V
SOUTH AFRICA

THE PROTAGONISTS

Michael Atherton
(Lancashire & England)
Aged 27. Captaining
England for the 26th
time in his 53rd Test,
which he started
with 4,084 runs in
Test cricket.

South Africa
Firm favourites for this
series, with a bowling
attack led by Allan
Donald, backed up by
Meyrick Pringle, Brian
McMillan and the
young Shaun Pollock
in his second Test and
also the slow-left armer,
Clive Eksteen.

MICHAEL ATHERTON

SOUTH AFRICA'S ALLAN DONALD

The Jo'burg resistance

Second Test · Johannesburg · December 3 & 4, 1995

*No one ever accused Michael Atherton of being an easy wicket. But even
his greatest admirers cannot have expected this epic 11-hour captain's innings
to save a game that most other batsmen would have given up as a lost cause*

They call the Wanderers ground in Johannesburg 'the Bull Ring'. The stands at either end rise vertically, creating an intimidating arena for an opposition batsman facing the might of South Africa's bowling attack. At a quarter past twelve on December 3, 1995, Mike Atherton, England's captain, and Alec Stewart walked down the long sloping wire-encased tunnel on to that stage with an apparently impossible task ahead of them. England had been set 479 to win, or more realistically had been left five sessions plus a quarter of an hour to survive to save the match. South Africans did not expect them to manage either.

It was England's first Test series in South Africa for 31

years. Since their re-entry to world cricket four years before, South Africans had become increasingly confident of their high standing. The century by Graeme Hick after England had been put in in the First Test had not been in their script, but the High Veldt rain had battered Centurion Park and the match had not progressed beyond the first innings.

This was the Second Test. South Africa, too, had found a century-maker after being put in to bat. Gary Kirsten had made 110, but Dominic Cork with five wickets and Devon Malcolm with four, with Jack Russell taking six catches, had kept England very much in the match and South Africa had been dismissed on the second morning for 332. Their disappointment at that had been alleviated by the sight of Atherton's off stump being removed by Allan Donald in his second over.

Though Stewart made 45, Graham Thorpe 34 and Robin Smith 52, England had been all out within the day for 200. After Donald had taken the first two wickets, the slow left-armer Clive Eksteen had taken three and Shaun Pollock in his second Test had polished off the tail with three more. South Africa were batting again on the second day, 132 runs ahead. Hansie Cronje, Daryl Cullinan and Jonty Rhodes had all contributed to driving home the advantage and the coup de grâce was provided by Brian McMillan. Cork had taken four more wickets for nine in the match and Russell's five catches had taken him to a Test record eleven.

Waiting for McMillan to reach his century on the fourth morning, following a cautious acceptance of an offer of bad light the previous evening, had probably delayed the declaration slightly over what would have been ideal for Cronje. But surely it could not make any difference. The pitch was cracked and unpredictable and the remaining ten-and-a-quarter hours of the match stretched ahead as Atherton and Stewart were now walking out in the face of that daunting task to be confronted by a crowd of 30,000, most of whom expected them to fail and were looking forward to seeing it happen.

They survived the opening burst of Donald and Meyrick Pringle, but in mid-afternoon McMillan made a double breakthrough, bowling both Stewart and the new batsman, Mark Ramprakash, with yorkers in the space of three balls. England were 75 for 2. By lunch, they had posted the

Atherton steers the ball away – and his team toward safety

Congratulations from Robin Smith as Atherton reaches a well-judged century

Congratulations from Robin Smith as Atherton reaches a well-judged century

'Over the years, I have really enjoyed my battles with Mike Atherton, because he stretches you as a bowler. You've got to earn his wicket, bowl him out, because he rarely gives it away with a misjudgement.'

ALLAN DONALD
(BELOW)

had reached 99. Atherton belongs to an elite club of those who have twice been out on 99 in Test cricket. He very nearly made that a unique feat of three times as he fended a short ball from Donald to the waiting hands of Gary Kirsten at short leg, who dropped the catch. Donald responded with another short one next ball and this time it was hooked for four, not only bringing up his ninth Test hundred, but also taking him past 4,000 Test runs.

Followers of England among the onlookers were now just about beginning to allow themselves the belief that this match might, after all, be saved, when Smith cut at Donald, got a top edge and the ball flew, with the speed of the bowling, to deep third man, where Pollock took the catch. Smith was out for 44 and England had lost their fifth wicket at 232. There were still almost three-quarters of an hour to go before lunch. The new batsman was Jack Russell.

The door was ajar and South Africa could scent victory. Frustratingly for them, they saw McMillan clutch in vain at a return chance from Russell when he had only made five.

The fielders were clustered round and very vocal. But Jack Russell was the ideal man for the situation, and he was not one to allow such a let-off to bother him. Playing his extravagant late 'leave' of the ball, to frustrate the bowlers by moving the bat sideways out of the line of the ball at the last possible second, he seemed to give more thought to keeping his captain going than in scoring any runs for himself. He could frequently be seen cajoling and encouraging the tiring Atherton. He reminded Atherton that he had battled five years before for over four hours against the West Indies in Barbados and still lost the match. He made it clear that he was not keen to repeat that disappointment.

Through the afternoon they defied all that could be thrown at them. Atherton passed his 150, while Russell in the two-hour session added only eight runs. But, importantly, they were still there at tea.

Gradually the abrasive comments of the close fielders had become noticeably quieter in the ears of those who could hear the pitch microphones. In the final session they had all but ceased.

At half past four, with the pair still together, the umpires announced the start of the last 15 overs. Atherton was 178 and at last the end was in sight. He must not now lose his

hundred and Atherton was 39. The pitch was playing better than expected and it was half an hour after tea before he lost his third-wicket partner, when he had made 67. Thorpe was the man to go, LBW as he played forward to Pringle. Six overs later Donald struck, to claim Hick as his 100th Test wicket, when he was caught behind for four.

Robin Smith, back in his native South Africa as an England player, was coming in now at 145 for 4 – the last specialist batsman. In the hour they had to weather before the close of that fourth day, Smith and Atherton added another 22 runs, but more importantly survived 14 more overs. Atherton had already batted nearly five hours to be 82 not out and England were 167 for 4.

It took a little while on the final morning for Atherton to slip back into the groove that had kept him going the previous day. He reached the nineties just before the new ball was taken, 11 overs into the day. Four overs later he incredible concentration. Nor would Russell let him. Run-scoring had all but ceased. Seven came in nine overs, at which point the third new ball was taken. But Donald was spent and there were only four overs left anyway.

Still Mike Atherton recalls a feeling of disbelieving relief when Hansie Cronje approached with hand outstretched to mark the end with one over still to go. The match had been drawn.

Atherton punched the air and beamed. He had batted 643 minutes for his 185 not out. It was the fourth-longest innings in Test history. He had faced 492 balls, 28 of which he had hit for four. Scarcely less remarkable was Jack Russell's innings of 29 from 235 balls in 4 hours 36 minutes (the *Times* correspondent noted that he was heading for a 17-hour century) and together they had added 119 and survived 75 overs.

South African spectators would have to overcome their natural disappointment before they could appreciate that they had witnessed one of the great innings – and certainly one of the greatest escape acts – of all time. The series, though, would be decided in South Africa's favour a month later by an England collapse in Cape Town.

England's warriors share the Man of the Match Champagne

South Africa v England

New Wanderers Stadium, Johannesburg, South Africa
England won the toss and fielded

30.11.1995 - 4.12.1995
Match Drawn

South Africa	1st innings		2nd innings	
A.C.Hudson	c Stewart b Cork	0	c Russell b Fraser	17
G.Kirsten	c Russel b Malcolm	110	c Russell b Malcolm	1
*W.J.Cronje	c Russell b Cork	35	c Russell b Cork	48
D.J.Cullinan	c Russell b Hick	69	c Gough b Cork	61
J.N.Rhodes	c Russell b Cork	5	c Russell b Fraser	57
B.M.McMillan	lbw b Cork	35	not out	100
+D.J.Richardson	c Russell b Malcolm	0	c Ramprakash b Malcolm	23
S.M.Pollock	c Smith b Malcolm	33	lbw b Cork	5
C.E.Eksteen	c Russell b Cork	13	c Russell b Cork	2
M.W.Pringle	not out	10	c Hick b Fraser	2
A.A.Donald	b Malcolm	0	not out	9
Extras	(b-1, lb-14, w-2, nb-5)	22	(b-5, lb-12, w-1, nb-3)	21
TOTAL	(all out)	**332**	(for 9 wickets declared)	**346**

Fall of Wickets	1-3	2-74	3-211	4-221	5-260		1-7	2-29	3-116	4-145	5-244
	6-260	7-278	8-314	9-331	10-332		6-296	7-304	8-311	9-314	

Bowling Analysis	O	M	R	W		O	M	R	W
D.G.Cork	32	7	84	5		31.3	6	78	4
D.E.Malcolm	22	5	62	4		13	2	65	2
A.R.C.Fraser	20	5	69	0		29	6	84	3
D.Gough	15	2	64	0		12	2	48	0
G.A.Hick	15	1	38	1		15	3	35	0
M.R.Ramprakash	4	0	19	0					

England	1st innings		2nd innings	
*M.A.Atherton	b Donald	9	not out	185
A.J.Stewart	c Kirsten b Pringle	45	b McMillan	38
M.R.Ramprakash	b Donald	4	b McMillan	0
G.P.Thorpe	c Kirsten b Eksteen	34	lbw b Pringle	17
G.A.Hick	c & b Eksteen	6	c Richardson b Donald	4
R.A.Smith	c & b McMillan	52	c Pollock b Donald	44
+R.C.Russell	c Rhodes b Eksteen	12	not out	29
D.G.Cork	c Cullinan b Pollock	8		
D.Gough	c & b Pollock	2		
A.R.C.Fraser	lbw b Pollock	0		
D.E.Malcolm	not out	0		
Extras	(b-6, lb-1, w-0, nb-21)	28	(b-4, lb-7, w-0, nb-23)	34
TOTAL	(all out)	**200**	(for 5 wickets)	**351**

Fall of Wickets	1-10	2-45	3-109	4-116	5-125		1-75	2-75	3-134	4-145	5-232
	6-147	7-178	8-193	9-200	10-200						

Bowling Analysis	O	M	R	W		O	M	R	W
A.A.Donald	15	3	49	2		35	9	95	2
M.W.Pringle	17	4	46	1		23	5	52	1
S.M.Pollock	15	2	44	3		29	11	65	0
B.M.McMillan	10.3	0	42	1		21	0	50	2
C.E.Eksteen	11	5	12	3		52	20	76	0
W.J.Cronje	3	1	2	0					
G.Kirsten	2	2	0	0					

Umpires: M J Kitchen, R S Dunne   **Man of the Match:** M A Atherton & R C Russell

NASSER HUSSAIN'S ANALYSIS

'The Atherton stubborn streak would have crept in'

'One big thing in Michael's favour was that he was accompanied by the loony, Jack.'

This was a hopeless situation. Five wickets down, 256 behind, just the tail to come. But the more hopeless it looks, the less you feel under pressure – not that Atherton feels pressure very much anyway.

His attitude would have been: "We're really up against it, I've been here before with England and I've got nothing to lose." He always says it was a very good Test wicket, so he felt he could get runs there. And the longer he batted, the more the Atherton stubborn streak would have crept in.

I've watched Atherton since he was 11 or 12 and he has always enjoyed just being out there and not giving his wicket away. The length of time that he occupied the crease would actually

have pleased him more than the score he got, because it would have been a record for him. And anyone who has been around for a while – Atherton, Stewart, Gooch – although they don't like to admit it, they love setting records. My longest innings was at Durban in 1999, and Alec Stewart kept me going by saying: "You've got an hour-and-a-half, an hour, to go past Atherton." I was 11 minutes short when it rained and I had to declare!

One big thing in Michael's favour was that he was accompanied by the loony, Jack, which is perfect. The last person you want for a partner when you are fatigued and running out of mental concentration is some nervous young lad who you have to help

NASSER HUSSAIN'S ANALYSIS

'When you're batting with Jack, and you meet in the middle between overs, he always has to tap the wicket and hit your pad before he walks off. Every over for all those overs. I can imagine Atherton having a little chuckle about it...'

through. Atherton would only have had so much left to give, so to see Russell coming in would have lifted him.

It would also have been amusing, because Jack has so many comical little routines when he's batting. For instance, when you meet in the middle between overs he has to tap the wicket and hit your pad before he walks off. So for all those hours they were batting together, every over Jack has to make sure he hits Mike's pad, and I can imagine Atherton turning away and having a little chuckle to himself.

Jack's a great ally in a fight. He's a huge patriot, so he'd be saying: "Let's do this for England." Johannesburg is known as the Bull Ring – it's a magnificent stadium – and those two

**'Let's do this for England...'
Jack Russell gives Atherton a pep talk**

NASSER HUSSAIN'S ANALYSIS

'If I'm playing Athers in a county game, I'll just keep quiet and ask him about his fishing in the hope that he'll get bored and nick a wide one…'

'The length of time that he occupied the crease would actually have pleased him more than the score he got, because it would have been a record for him…'

They shall not pass: Jack Russell shows a dead bat to the South African attack, scoring just 29 runs from 235 balls

NASSER HUSSAIN'S ANALYSIS

'Anyone who has been around for a while – Atherton, Stewart, Gooch – although they don't like to admit it, they love setting records.'

would have felt like gladiators, trying to keep England in the game and in the series. They were the perfect partnership.

Peter Baxter noticed that the South Africans got quieter as Atherton's innings went on, but I think they admire him so much now that they don't even bother chirping him. They almost feel that it wakes him up and makes him more stubborn. If I'm playing Athers in a county game, I'll just keep quiet and ask him about his fishing in the hope that he'll get bored and nick a wide one…

When we toured South Africa in 1999/2000, it was the first time Atherton had been back to Johannesburg, and he

was dreading it. From the moment we landed, everyone wanted to talk about his innings. We went to a dinner at the Wanderers ground and all the speakers mentioned it, along with the Atherton/Donald shootout at Trent Bridge, and how they felt that decision had cost them the series.

It's very difficult when you return to the scene of your best innings, because you know that however well you play, you're not going to match it, and I could see that Atherton wasn't looking forward to the game. It was no coincidence that he got a beauty in each innings and bagged it. That's just cricket's way of taking you down a peg or two.

TREVOR BAILEY & WILLIE WATSON
V
AUSTRALIA

Willie Watson
(Yorkshire & England)
Aged 33. Playing his seventh Test, having played his first when he was 31. Since then he had made 258 runs. He also won four caps for England at football.

Trevor Bailey
(Essex & England)
Aged 29. Playing his 16th Test, he had previously made 689 runs and taken 42 wickets and would go on to make that record 2,290 runs and 132 wickets in 61 Tests.

Australia
Led by Lindsay Hassett with one of the great fast-bowling attacks in Ray Lindwall and Keith Miller, supported by Bill Johnston and the left arm Alan Davidson and with two good leg spinners in Richie Benaud and Doug Ring.

TREVOR BAILEY

WILLIE WATSON

AUSTRALIA'S LINDSAY HASSETT

Barnacle Bailey digs in

Second Test • Lord's • June 30, 1953

Trevor Bailey was the world's most boring batsman – and proud of it. When it came to saving a game, no one could match The Barnacle. At Lord's in June 1953, there was rather more than a game at stake. Save this one, and Bailey and Watson knew they might yet regain the Ashes

The month that opened with the splendour of the Coronation of the new Queen Elizabeth ended with a heroic example of the bulldog spirit as two Englishmen battled it out at Lord's. Australia had held the Ashes for 19 years, but now Bradman had gone. The two fast bowlers who had been his spearhead in 1948, Lindwall

and Miller, were still there, however, in a side led by Lindsay Hassett. The First Test had been drawn thanks to rain, with England tantalisingly needing 109 more to win with nine wickets in hand, after Alec Bedser had taken 14 wickets in the match. For the Second Test, England captain Len Hutton persuaded the chairman of selectors, Freddie

Essex all-rounder Trevor Bailey practises his sternest defence in the nets in 1955, while Willie Watson limbers up in 1956, shortly after he gave up playing football to concentrate on cricket. Watson, who played for Huddersfield and Sunderland, had gone to the 1950 World Cup in Brazil – but it cost him over £250 in lost wages from Yorkshire. David Beckham would never believe it!

Brown, to pick himself. Lord's was full well before Hassett won the toss and went out to open the innings. He made his second hundred in successive Tests as Australia made 346. Bedser had taken five wickets this time. Hutton echoed his opposite number with a century – 145 – which took him into the third day. He was supported by 78 from Tom Graveney and 57 from Denis Compton, which enabled England to take a first-innings lead of 26.

A blow from Brian Statham early on in Keith Miller's innings – and boos from the crowd when he dropped his bat – seemed to concentrate his effort. His century took him an untypical five hours, then the Australians pushed on to give themselves time to bowl England out. Some lusty blows from Ray Lindwall did the job. Australia were all out, with an hour to go on the fourth day, for 368, leaving England 343 to win in five minutes under seven hours.

The way that 42-year-old Freddie Brown had spun his leg breaks made England aware that there would be danger from the leg spin of Doug Ring and Richie Benaud – but in a burst of five rapid overs it was Ray Lindwall who reduced them to 12 for 3. Eight more runs came before the close, but the speculation overnight came to only one conclusion. Australia would win the Test on the morrow.

Trevor Bailey, on his way up from Southend on the train

'When I joined Willie my sole objective was still to be there at lunch. My approach was to assume that every ball was potentially lethal and had to be stopped.'

TREVOR BAILEY,
'WICKETS, CATCHES
AND THE ODD RUN'

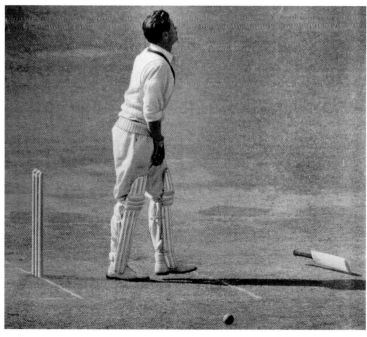

Ouch! Trevor Bailey rubs his left hand after nearly catching a Neil Harvey hook at short leg; Keith Miller drops his bat after being hit where it hurts by Brian Statham; and Ray Lindwall showing how he took five wickets in England's first innings. Opposite: Bailey plays a rare attacking shot during his Lord's vigil

to Fenchurch Street in the morning, was taken aback to read such sentiments in the papers. He was next man in, to follow the overnight pair of Willie Watson and Denis Compton. He did concede that the odds were against England, but felt it a little premature to write them off. The public, though, had agreed with the press and the crowd had diminished for what most felt would be the last rites.

The usually crucial first hour was negotiated safely, but soon afterwards Australia took the wicket they wanted most. Bill Johnston had Compton LBW for 33. It was 73 for 4 and the Australians showed clearly that they felt the game was as good as won. But Trevor Bailey's reputation as 'the barnacle' was already forged and he came in with an attitude of total defence – his bat as dead as he could make it.

Bailey relished such a challenge. With no chance of England winning the match, he knew what he had to do. Watson, the partner he came in to join, was a quiet fellow – less obviously defiant, but prepared to bat the day out with patience. The character contrasts showed in the fact that, when they had reached the first milestone of the lunch interval, Bailey ate both his own and Watson's lunch.

By that time they were 116 for 4, with Watson 54 and Bailey, after 40 minutes' batting, 10. After lunch they were

treated to the two leg spinners in harness, but Hassett felt the need to bring back his seam bowlers before the second new ball was available and Bailey felt that that helped them to weather its onslaught. The first half-hour with it in the hands of Miller and Lindwall produced only six runs, and the frustrated Hassett turned back to his spinners.

So confident was Watson now, that he recalls going up to Bailey and asking him if he thought they should be chasing the runs. Bailey just turned his back and walked away.

They were still there at tea with the score now 183 for 4; Watson 84 and Bailey 39. It sounds attritional fare, but the story is told of the rugby international who had only gone to Lord's for the beer, but was nevertheless so wrapped up in the tenseness of the drama that he failed for two hours to notice that he had kicked over his pint.

The left-arm Davidson joined Miller in the attack after tea, but first Bailey reached his fifty after three hours and forty minutes and then Watson a well-deserved century, with his 14th four. He lasted another 25 minutes before he edged Ring to first slip and, after five-and-three-quarter hours, his long vigil came to an end for 109.

He and Bailey had added 163 together, but more importantly had held up Australia for over four hours.

A score of 236 for 5 soon became 246 for 6 as Bailey for once went for a more extravagant drive off Ring and was caught by Benaud in the covers. After taking England so close to salvation with his 71, he berated himself all the way back to the pavilion. For the Australians the door was ajar again, with the veteran Brown, who had had his pads on all day, and the perky Godfrey Evans now in, half an hour to go and only Wardle, Bedser and Statham to come.

Trevor Bailey found that half-hour more agonising than all his time at the crease. But Brown was a good player of spin, which was now Hassett's ploy, with fielders crowded round the bat, and Australia did not take another wicket until the last over, when Brown edged Benaud to slip. Wardle kept the last few balls out and the match was drawn.

The two evenly-matched sides were to play two more draws, not unaffected by the weather, before the celebrated recapture of the Ashes by England at The Oval – made possible by the determination of Watson and Bailey.

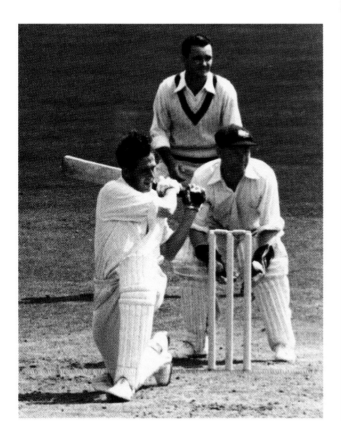

England v Australia

Lord's, London, England
Australia won the toss and batted

25.6.1953 - 30.6.1953
Match Drawn

Australia	1st innings		2nd innings	
*A.L.Hassett	c Bailey b Bedser	104	c Evans b Statham	3
A.R.Morris	st. Evans b Bedser	30	c Statham b Compton	89
R.N.Harvey	lbw b Bedser	59	(4) b Bedser	21
K.R.Miller	b Wardle	25	(3) b Wardle	109
G.B.Hole	c Compton b Wardle	13	lbw b Brown	47
R.Benaud	lbw b Wardle	0	c Graveney b Bedser	5
A.K.Davidson	c Statham b Bedser	76	c & b Brown	15
D.T.Ring	lbw b Wardle	18	lbw b Brown	7
R.R.Lindwall	b Statham	9	b Bedser	50
+G.R.A.Langley	c Watson b Bedser	1	b Brown	9
W.A.Johnston	not out	3	not out	0
Extras	(b-4, lb-4, w-0, nb-0)	8	(b-8, lb-5, w-0, nb-0)	13
TOTAL	(all out)	**346**	(all out)	**368**

Fall of Wickets	1-65	2-190	3-225	4-229	5-240	1-3	2-168	3-227	4-235	5-248
	6-280	7-291	8-330	9-331	10-346	6-296	7-305	8-308	9-362	10-368

Bowling Analysis	O	M	R	W		O	M	R	W
A.V.Bedser	42.4	8	105	5		31.5	8	77	3
J.B.Statham	28	7	48	1		15	3	40	1
F.R.Brown	25	7	53	0		27	4	82	4
T.E.Bailey	16	2	55	0		10	4	24	0
J.H.Wardle	29	8	77	4		46	18	111	1
D.C.S.Compton	3	0	21	1					

England	1st innings		2nd innings	
*L.Hutton	c Hole b Johnston	145	c Hole b Lindwall	5
D.Kenyon	c Davidson b Lindwall	3	c Hassett b Lindwall	2
T.W.Graveney	b Lindwall	78	c Langley b Johnston	2
D.C.S.Compton	c Hole b Benaud	57	lbw b Johnston	33
W.Watson	st. Langley b Johnston	4	c Hole b Ring	109
T.E.Bailey	c & b Miller	2	c Benaud b Ring	71
F.R.Brown	c Langley b Lindwall	22	c Hole b Benaud	28
+T.G.Evans	b Lindwall	0	not out	11
J.H.Wardle	b Davidson	23	not out	0
A.V.Bedser	b Lindwall	1		
J.B.Statham	not out	17		
Extras	(b-11, lb-1, w-1, nb-7)	20	(b-7, lb-6, w-2, nb-6)	21
TOTAL	(all out)	**372**	(for 7 wickets)	**282**

Fall of Wickets	1-9	2-177	3-279	4-291	5-301	1-6	2-10	3-12	4-73	5-236
	6-328	7-328	8-332	9-341	10-372	6-246	7-282			

Bowling Analysis	O	M	R	W		O	M	R	W
R.R.Lindwall	23	4	66	5		19	3	26	2
K.R.Miller	25	6	57	1		17	8	17	0
W.A.Johnston	35	11	91	2		29	10	70	2
D.T.Ring	14	2	43	0		29	5	84	2
R.Benaud	19	4	70	1		17	6	51	1
A.K.Davidson	10.5	2	25	1		14	5	13	0
G.B.Hole	1	1	0	0					

Umpires: H.G.Baldwin, F.S.Lee

NASSER HUSSAIN'S ANALYSIS

'England fans love a good, defiant rearguard action'

'Today's players would find it amazing that Trevor Bailey got the train in from Southend in the middle of a Test match.'

'A different world...' Trevor Bailey films Colin Cowdrey, Frank Tyson and Denis Compton on England's 1956 voyage to South Africa

It's interesting that there were so many great names in that England team – Compton, Hutton, Graveney, Bedser – and yet the heroes of the hour were Bailey and Watson who, with all due respect, were obviously not such big stars. Trevor probably dined out on that for many years.

But the fact that Barnacle Bailey's epic resistance has become a legend is also indicative of how we in England view our sporting heroes. When it comes to a choice between dogged determination and flamboyant charisma, English cricket supporters love the two extremes.

I get umpteen letters complaining that we haven't got any Graveneys or Comptons any more. I think Darren Gough approaches that extreme, with his exuberant character, and the supporters love that sort of player as long as he does

well – but they don't like it if the guy has all that talent and doesn't make the most of it.

At the same time, especially in certain parts of the world such as Yorkshire, supporters love the other side of the coin – the grit of a Boycott or an Atherton. They love to see people fighting for their lives, even if they haven't got all the ability. There's nothing England fans like better than a good, defiant rearguard action such as Michael Atherton's innings in Johannesburg. That's why the British public love Jack Russell: he's a fighter. When Graham Gooch played some of those innings with the ball flying all over the place and he was seeing England home, he became much more popular than when he was smacking a quick 200 at Southend, because it shows a bit of guts and steel.

This is the subject we have had the most letters about

NASSER HUSSAIN'S ANALYSIS

'Nothing hurts me more than people saying that England don't show fight and character.'

Trevor Bailey watches as Ray Lindwall fires in a thunderbolt at The Oval, where England clinched a dramatic Ashes series

over the past two or three years – "Come on, show some fight." You know the players do fight. That has been the case in all the teams I've played in, with the odd exception. When you are collapsing, you are trying to show fight – but it just doesn't come across that way. Nothing hurts me more than people saying that England don't show fight and character. On the 1999/2000 tour of South Africa and Zimbabwe, we did show that we were going to go out there and not just roll over, and we received more positive letters than for a long time.

Some of the minor details in this story show how much the game has changed. Today's players, who spend Test matches holed up together in a hotel, would find it amazing that Trevor Bailey got the train in from Southend in the middle of a Test. "What are you doing this morning, Trevor?" "Oh, I'm off to face Lindwall, Miller and Benaud at Lord's."

Then you have the England captain encouraging the chairman of selectors to pick himself! He obviously must have wanted to keep his job as captain.

I love the story of Bailey eating Watson's lunch, though you do wonder if these things have been exaggerated. At one time Trevor was both the captain and secretary of Essex *and* cricket correspondent of the *Financial Times*. The story goes that he used to leave the field at tea-time to go up to the secretary's office and count the takings then write his *FT* report while still keeping an eye on play in case he had to make a decision. It really was a different world.

JACK HOBBS & HERBERT SUTCLIFFE
V
AUSTRALIA

THE PROTAGONISTS

Jack Hobbs
(Surrey & England)
Aged 46. Playing his
53rd Test, having made
4,696 runs. He would
finish in 1930 with
5,410 runs, a record
3,636 of them against
Australia. He became
the first professional
cricketer to be
knighted.

Herbert Sutcliffe
(Yorkshire & England)
Aged 34. Playing his
26th Test, having been
Hobbs' opening partner
18 times. He started the
Test with 2,173 runs
and finished his career
with 4,555 runs from
54 Tests.

Australia
Not at their strongest.
Captained by Jack
Ryder, with the young
Bradman playing his
second Test, but they
did have one truly
great bowler in
Clarrie Grimmett.

JACK HOBBS

HERBERT SUTCLIFFE

AUSTRALIA'S JACK RYDER

Battling on a sticky wicket

Third Test · Melbourne · January 4 & 5, 1929

*Sometimes in cricket the battle is as much against the conditions as the opposition.
The weather on the sixth day of 1929's timeless Test at Melbourne did its best to conspire
against England. But in Hobbs and Sutcliffe the visitors had a legendary opening partnership
who relished the opportunity to show that they could prevail even against the elements*

It was a battle against overwhelming odds that could not happen in the modern game for two reasons. It was fought over the sixth and seventh days of a Test match, because all Tests in Australia between the two World Wars were timeless – to be played to a finish. The circumstances that made it such a remarkable achievement arose from the fact that pitches then remained uncovered throughout a match and this one had become a 'sticky'.

England went into this Third Test having already won at Brisbane and Sydney. It began on December 29, 1928, with Jack Ryder winning the toss for Australia. Ryder made a century, as did Alan Kippax. The young Don Bradman,

Jack Hobbs and Herbert Sutcliffe, the most famous opening partnership in cricket, who passed 100 together 26 times

after being left out at Sydney, returned for his second Test and made 79 in a total of 397.

England lost Hobbs for 20 late on the second day but Wally Hammond, following 251 in the previous Test, went on to make 200 which, with only Sutcliffe and Jardine apart from him passing fifty, was responsible for England taking a first-innings lead of 20.

By the fifth morning, Australia were 143 for 4 when the 20-year-old Don Bradman began his fourth Test innings. Bill Woodfull reached his hundred after lunch and then, on an oppressively hot and sticky afternoon,

'My diary has the note: "We did not think we had an earthly." I realised, after an hour's batting, that we had a chance, if we did not lose too many wickets that afternoon, as the wicket was drying fast.'

JACK HOBBS, 'MY LIFE STORY'

with the predicament they had found themselves in. Melbourne had the reputation of being possibly the most difficult pitch in the world as it dried after rain. A lot of water had fallen on the bulli soil used here in pitch preparation, and now a hot sun had returned, so that England would have to bat on a drying pitch. The effect of that was to produce sharp and unpredictable lift from the ball.

Jack Hobbs and Herbert Sutcliffe came out to open the innings with time for two overs before lunch. They negotiated those, but soon after the interval, with

with Larwood struggling in the England attack with a pulled muscle, Bradman went on to his first Test century.

He was eventually out for 112. At the close of play Australia, at 347 for 8, were 327 runs ahead. And that night, as the teams were dining in various parts of Melbourne, they heard the thunderstorm break and knew that, as that heavy rain was falling on an uncovered pitch, Australia's position was becoming well-nigh impregnable.

It rained through the night and delayed the start of the sixth day, but eventually White was able to polish off the Australian innings for the addition of only four more runs. England would need 332 to win – but they would need to get them on a Melbourne 'sticky'.

Jack Hobbs, who had recently celebrated his 46th birthday and so had seen it all, remarked to the playwright Ben Travers, who was travelling with the team, that he thought England might well be all out by tea, and wrote later of the friends who came round to express sympathy

the score only 10, Hobbs was lucky to escape as a ball from Edward a'Beckett lifted to take the shoulder of the bat, but was missed in the slips. No one doubted that there would be other chances aplenty. In later years, Herbert Sutcliffe wrote and broadcast about that batting experience:

"Everyone said that if England scored as many as sixty, they'd be doing extremely well. Before lunch that wicket was a nightmare. By three in the afternoon, with the hot sun on it, it was a terrifying, vicious, murderous thing, ten times worse. The ball popped up quite vertically and all we could do was keep our bats out of the way and take the rising ball on the body. At the end we were black and blue with bruises."

Sir Don Bradman, witnessing then "my first exhibition of what English batsmen can do on a sticky wicket", wrote in his autobiographical *Farewell to Cricket*, "Even now I think Sutcliffe's exhibition that day was the nearest approach to mastery on a sticky wicket I saw throughout

Heroes of the Twenties: Hobbs, Sutcliffe and Clarrie Grimmett. Right: The final scoreboard

my career. Hobbs, of course, was renowned for his skill under such conditions … but none … to my mind quite equalled Sutcliffe, whose uncanny ability to let the ball go when it jumped or turned was simply amazing."

The *Times* correspondent gave the prize the other way: "To Hobbs must be awarded the palm. He could not be caught by any tricks; his footwork was superb; and he showed younger and possibly more active players how it was possible to change the stroke almost at the last minute and still make it technically correct."

The ball was stopping, leaping and often turning sharply, so that in this game of survival it is quite remarkable that they had reached 85 by the tea interval and were still together. Hobbs, by virtue of age and huge reputation very much the senior pro, advised his captain, Percy Chapman, that if either he or Sutcliffe got out in the final session, Douglas Jardine, suitably determined and technically adept, should come in next in order to try to save Hammond for the next day.

After an opening partnership of 105, it was Hobbs who went, LBW to the off spinner Don Blackie for 49. But there was no other wicket for the increasingly frustrated Australian bowlers that night. At the close Sutcliffe was 83 not out and England 171 for 1. It had been, in Sutcliffe's own words, "a cricket miracle".

The worst of the devils had gone next day, though batting was still not easy. Sutcliffe reached his century just before lunch, which was taken at 222 for 2. Hammond was run out for 32, and Patsy Hendren now played some more aggressive shots to see them to within 14 runs of the target – at which point, after nearly six-and-a-half hours' batting, Sutcliffe was LBW to Clarrie Grimmett for 135.

A mini-collapse followed, which must have given the Australians a ray of hope – three more wickets falling to make it 328 for 7 – but Geary and Duckworth saw England home by three wickets.

One of the most remarkable cricket escapes had secured the Ashes for England. The Prime Minister, Stanley Baldwin, sent the team a congratulatory telegram but, as they celebrated, the players could not have believed that it would be 68 years before another England side would successfully chase a target in excess of 300.

Australia v England

MCG, Melbourne, Australia
Australia won the toss and batted

29.12.1928 - 5.1.1929
England won by 3 wickets

Australia	1st innings		2nd innings	
W.M.Woodfull	c Jardine b Tate	7	c Duckworth b Tate	107
V.Y.Richardson	c Duckworth b Larwood	3	b Larwood	5
H.S.T.L.Hendry	c Jardine b Larwood	23	st. Duckworth b White	12
A.F.Kippax	c Jardine b Larwood	100	b Tate	41
*J.Ryder	c Hendren b Tate	112	b Geary	5
D.G.Bradman	b Hammond	79	c Duckworth b Geary	112
+W.A.S.Oldfield	b Geary	3	b White	7
E.L.a'Beckett	c Duckworth b White	41	b White	6
R.K.Oxenham	b Geary	15	b White	39
C.V.Grimmett	c Duckworth b Geary	5	not out	4
D.D.Blackie	not out	2	b White	0
Extras	(b-4, lb-3, w-0, nb-0)	7	(b-6, lb-7, w-0, nb-0)	13
TOTAL	(all out)	**397**	(all out)	**351**

Fall of Wickets: 1-5 2-15 3-57 4-218 5-282 6-287 7-373 8-387 9-394 10-397
1-7 2-60 3-138 4-143 5-201 6-226 7-252 8-345 9-351 10-351

Bowling Analysis	O	M	R	W	O	M	R	W
H.Larwood	37	3	127	3	16	3	37	1
M.W.Tate	46	17	87	2	47	15	70	2
G.Geary	31.5	4	83	3	30	4	94	2
W.R.Hammond	8	4	19	1	16	6	30	0
J.C.White	57	30	64	1	56.5	20	107	5
D.R.Jardine	1	0	10	0				

England	1st innings		2nd innings	
J.B.Hobbs	c Oldfield b a'Beckett	20	lbw b Blackie	49
H.Sutcliffe	b Blackie	58	lbw b Grimmett	135
W.R.Hammond	c a'Beckett b Blackie	200	(4) run out	32
*A.P.F.Chapman	b Blackie	24	(6) c Woodfull b Ryder	5
E.H.Hendren	c a'Beckett b Hendry	19	b Oxenham	45
D.R.Jardine	c & b Blackie	62	(3) b Grimmett	33
H.Larwood	c & b Blackie	0		
G.Geary	LBW b Grimmett	1	not out	4
M.W.Tate	c Kippax b Grimmett	21	(7) run out	0
+G.Duckworth	b Blackie	3	(9) not out	0
J.C.White	not out	8		
Extras	(b-1, lb-0, w-0, nb-0)	1	(b-15, lb-14, w-0, nb-0)	29
TOTAL	(all out)	**417**	(for 7 wickets)	**332**

Fall of Wickets: 1-28 2-161 3-201 4-238 5-364 6-364 7-381 8-385 9-391 10-417
1-105 2-199 3-257 4-318 5-326 6-328 7-328

Bowling Analysis	O	M	R	W	O	M	R	W
E.L.a'Beckett	37	7	92	1	22	5	39	0
H.S.T.L.Hendry	20	8	35	1	23	5	33	0
C.V.Grimmett	55	14	114	2	42	12	96	2
R.K.Oxenham	35	11	67	0	28	10	44	1
D.D.Blackie	44	13	94	6	39	11	75	1
J.Ryder	4	0	14	0	5.5	1	16	1

Umpires: D.A.Elder, G.A.Hele

CRICKET'S GREATEST BATTLES

NASSER HUSSAIN'S ANALYSIS

'It was obviously a case of sheer survival'

'It's a technique that can only come from experience, so it's no coincidence that at 46, Hobbs was good at playing on a sticky.'

Playing on a sticky dog takes a rare technique, and I think if you put most batsmen in the world today on a wicket like that, they would come unstuck immediately. I'm sure a lot of them would work it out eventually, but it's not a technique that batsmen need today. For Jack Hobbs and Herbert Sutcliffe it was obviously a case of sheer survival, because the next day the wicket got flatter.

The percentages on a sticky wicket are hugely in favour of one way of batting, which is something Hobbs and Sutcliffe must have understood well. If the ball's bouncing and spinning off a length, then square shots come into it more, such as the pull. The drive becomes a difficult shot and the leg side gets favoured a lot.

It's a technique that can only come from experience, so it's no coincidence that at the age of 46, Hobbs was pretty good at playing on a 'sticky'. Keith Fletcher mastered it, too, and I remember him advising me to go and play club cricket in Australia because the more different wickets you play on, the better you will become. In Fletcher's era, once play had started for the day, the pitch was left uncovered, and he says that some of the most difficult cricket he ever played was when he had to face Derek Underwood on a drying wicket.

The idea of covering pitches at all during a Test match came from Australia, because in the series after Bodyline, every match was decided by the weather and the team batting when the wicket got wet were the losers. This is a subject that Michael Atherton and I

'Keith Fletcher says that some of the most difficult cricket he ever played was when he had to face Derek Underwood on a drying wicket.'

The Master: Jack Hobbs in action and, opposite, relaxing with a cigarette after scoring his 2,000th run of the 1925 season

often argue about. He thinks we should go back to uncovered wickets because it will improve our batsmen's technique. But my argument is that it would be a completely different technique to what is required in modern Test cricket. There's no point us playing on sticky dogs here in England and then playing the West Indies on a hard, covered Test wicket. It might improve your technique for playing a ball that lifts off a length, but that's all.

My main complaint about county cricket is the wickets. I don't think it's a bad system or that the players are terrible –

but the wickets in England are unlike the rest of the world, so for half the year we are playing a different form of cricket. Our conditions are not like anywhere else. The balls don't help, either: in county cricket we use big hard Duke balls with big seams and in Tests we use smaller Kookaburra balls with soft seams. We might as well be playing football. When we go to India, Pakistan, Sri Lanka or the West Indies, it has nothing to do with what we do domestically.

I see that this was a timeless Test. If we had timeless Test matches now, England would have quite a few days off!

One moment in time

GATTING v WARNE · OLD TRAFFORD · 1993

BOYCOTT v HOLDING · BARBADOS · 1981

Opposite: The climax to the finest over of fast bowling ever seen.

This page: Ian Healy, Mike Gatting and Geoffrey Boycott

MIKE GATTING
V
SHANE WARNE

Mike Gatting
(Middlesex & England)
Two days before his
36th birthday. Former
England captain,
playing his 73rd Test.
Started it with 4,136
runs to his credit.

Shane Warne
(Victoria & Australia)
Aged 23. Playing his
12th Test, but his first
against England.
Previously with 31 Test
wickets, but would
more than double that
in this series.

MIKE GATTING

SHANE WARNE

'That Ball'

First Test • Old Trafford • June 4, 1993

The shortest battle in this book lasted just three-quarters of a second.
But it was probably the most significant three-quarters of a second
in recent cricket history…

Opposite: The moment
the young magician
announced his presence

The arrival of an Australian touring team in England always brings high anticipation. In 1993, much of that was centred on a 23-year-old from Victoria who purveyed that most intriguing of bowling arts – leg spin.

Peter Roebuck, in *The Cricketer*, introduced him thus: "Shane Warne first appeared as a bowler with chubby fingers disinclined to inhabit the dreary flatlands of the mildewed. So excited were the selectors to find a leg spinner that they picked him and kept on picking him, even though he was, at first, murdered by the Indian batsmen. Just 15 months on he is the best leg spinner in the world according to no less an authority than Martin Crowe."

Warne did not feature in the one-day internationals which preceded the Tests, but in four first-class matches

'That was the best ball I've ever bowled in Test cricket. I've probably watched it 2,000 times. It was lucky, to be honest. It was the first ball, a leg spinner. You're trying to feel comfortable, to get the ball on a length – and to warm up, because over here it can be a bit cold… Ian Healy jumped up, so I decided to jump up – I didn't really know what was happening – and it was only when Gatting actually started walking away that I saw he had been bowled. Healy came up to me and said: "That wasn't a bad delivery to start with." No, not bad.'

SHANE WARNE TALKING TO JOHN INVERDALE ON BBC TV'S 'ON SIDE'

England v Australia

Old Trafford, Manchester, England
England won the toss and fielded

3.6.1993 - 7.6.1993
Australia won by 179 runs

Australia	1st innings		2nd innings	
M.A.Taylor	c & b Such	124	lbw b Such	9
M.J.Slater	c Stewart b DeFreitas	58	c Caddick b Such	27
D.C.Boon	c Lewis b Such	21	c Gatting b DeFreitas	93
M.E.Waugh	c & b Tufnell	6	b Tufnell	64
*A.R.Border	st. Stewart b Such	17	c & b Caddick	31
S.R.Waugh	b Such	3	not out	78
+I.A.Healy	c Such b Tufnell	12	not out	102
B.P.Julian	c Gatting b Such	0		
M.G.Hughes	c DeFreitas b Such	2		
S.K.Warne	not out	15		
C.J.McDermott	run out	8		
Extras	(b-8, lb-8, w-0, nb-7)	23	(b-6, lb-14, w-8, nb-0)	28
TOTAL	(all out)	289	(for 5 wickets declared)	432

Fall of Wickets	1-128	2-183	3-221	4-225	5-232	1-23	2-46	3-155	4-234	5-252
	6-260	7-264	8-266	9-267	10-289					

Bowling Analysis	O	M	R	W	O	M	R	W
A.R.Caddick	15	4	38	0	20	3	79	1
P.A.J.DeFreitas	23	8	46	1	24	1	80	1
C.C.Lewis	13	2	44	0	9	0	43	0
P.M.Such	33.3	9	67	6	31	6	78	2
P.C.R.Tufnell	28	5	78	2	37	4	112	1
G.A.Hick	9	1	20	0				

England	1st innings		2nd innings	
*G.A.Gooch	c Julian b Warne	65	handled the ball	133
M.A.Atherton	c Healy b Hughes	19	c Taylor b Warne	25
M.W.Gatting	b Warne	4	b Hughes	23
R.A.Smith	c Taylor b Warne	4	b Warne	18
G.A.Hick	c Border b Hughes	34	c Healy b Hughes	22
+A.J.Stewart	b Julian	27	c Healy b Warne	11
C.C.Lewis	c Boon b Hughes	9	c Taylor b Warne	43
P.A.J.DeFreitas	lbw b Julian	5	lbw b Julian	7
A.R.Caddick	c Healy b Warne	7	c Warne b Hughes	25
P.M.Such	not out	14	c Border b Hughes	9
P.C.R.Tufnell	c Healy b Hughes	1	not out	0
Extras	(b-6, lb-10, w-0, nb-5)	21	(b-0, lb-11, w-1, nb-4)	16
TOTAL	(all out)	210	(all out)	332

Fall of Wickets	1-71	2-80	3-84	4-123	5-148	1-73	2-133	3-171	4-223	5-230
	6-168	7-178	8-183	9-203	10-210	6-238	7-260	8-299	9-331	10-332

Bowling Analysis	O	M	R	W	O	M	R	W
C.J.McDermott	18	2	50	0	30	9	76	0
M.G.Hughes	20.5	5	59	4	27.2	4	92	4
B.P.Julian	11	2	30	2	14	1	67	1
S.K.Warne	24	10	51	4	49	26	86	4
A.R.Border	1	0	4	0				

Umpires: H.D.Bird, K.E.Palmer   **Man of the Match:** S.K.Warne

against the counties he had taken 19 wickets. Wet weather before the First Test in Manchester had affected the pitch, and England's debutant off-spinner Peter Such enjoyed the result, taking six first-innings wickets to spin Australia out for 289. In reply, Graham Gooch and Michael Atherton put on 71 for the first England wicket, before Atherton was caught behind off Merv Hughes. In came Mike Gatting.

Enough had been written and spoken about the wiles of Warne that there was already chuntering round the ground about Allan Border's failure to try the spinner thus far. Maybe Border had more of a sense of the dramatic than we gave him credit for. Gatting had a celebrated belief that no spinner should be allowed to bowl unmolested at him – and very early in his innings he was going to get the chance to make his point.

The crowd cheered as the *wunderkind* was brought on to bowl. There were murmurs of approval in commentary boxes. Journalists paused at their laptops to observe the start of this phase of the game. Warne kept them waiting as he sorted his field out with his captain.

On *Test Match Special*, the commentator was Jonathan Agnew: "Now, there must be a little bit of pressure on young Warne's shoulders, I would think, here. Because he'll know that his team are expecting him to come on and take some wickets, or at least turn the ball.

"Here comes Shane Warne off only two or three paces. He bowls and Gatting is taken on the pad… He's bowled!

"Well, Gatting's still standing there. He can't believe it, but that must have turned a very long way. It took his off stump. Gatting can't believe it.

"That is Shane Warne's first delivery in a Test match in England. He's comprehensively bowled Mike Gatting. That must have turned an awful long way."

The ball had appeared to be drifting down the leg side. It pitched a foot wide of the stumps and Gatting clearly felt that no more than a perfunctory use of the pad was needed – if that. As it hit the off stump and Gatting froze in disbelief, the crowd, the Australian fielders and possibly even Warne himself could scarcely believe their eyes. For a split second there was a shocked silence and then came the roar.

A rueful Gatting said later that evening, "In 20 years, that ball will have pitched five feet outside leg to hit off."

MIKE GATTING V CRICKET'S GREATEST BATTLES SHANE WARNE · 1993

NASSER HUSSAIN'S ANALYSIS

'That moment has probably played on English batters' minds ever since'

A couple of years before this, I was playing club cricket in Australia and I remember watching this blond beach boy bowling in the Cricket Academy nets. He was really big – even bigger than he is now – and he looked like he should have been out posing with his surfboard. But there he was in the nets, day in day out, practising his leg breaks and his googlies and his flippers. I didn't know who he was, but I made a mental note of the name Shane Warne.

By the time he came to England, there had been a lot of build-up about him and everyone wanted to see what all the fuss was about. It was a useful wicket for him, an Old Trafford turner which the rain had made damp. Allan Border and Mark Taylor always used Warne very well: they never over-bowled him. So Border didn't bring him on too early.

What surprised many people about 'That Ball' was the drift. Because we don't see a lot of leg spin here, people think he just runs up, bowls the ball, pitches it and it turns. Whereas in leg spin the drift is very important. So it was a surprise for people to see the ball drift in from outside off stump towards the leg stump, making the batsman play the ball slightly to the leg side. And it would have been an even bigger surprise when it pitched outside leg stump and hit the top of off. It was particularly shocking because it was against Gatting, who was a very good player of spin.

Everything about it was absolutely brilliant. Gatt's look as it went past him and hit the stumps. Gatt standing there in disbelief. Healy leaping in the air, then running to congratulate Warne. Gatt still just standing there looking at his stumps. A classic moment of cricket.

That moment has probably played on English batters'

'It was particularly shocking because it was against Gatting, who was a very good player of spin.'

NASSER HUSSAIN'S ANALYSIS

'Everything about it was absolutely brilliant. Gatt's look as it went past him and hit the stumps. Gatt standing there in disbelief. Healy leaping in the air, then running to congratulate Warne. Gatt still just standing there looking at his stumps...'

Here it is again ... the most-replayed dismissal in cricket history. Sorry, Mike

minds ever since. We'd heard about the flippers and the googlies, but that was his orthodox leg spinner. If that's just his normal ball…

The word 'great' is used too much but Warne *is* a great bowler. When you face him, he is at you all the time. He rarely bowls a bad ball, and when he does it's to set you up for the flipper. So he'll drag one down and you'll cut him for four. The next ball follows the same trajectory and looks exactly the same; you think, "Oh, it's a long hop," so you go to cut it and before you can get your bat down it's bowled you. I remember Alec Stewart falling for it in Brisbane in 1994. Warne's shoulder operation in 1998 was a big loss to cricket, because he temporarily lost the flipper, and that was a magical ball.

Warne is also a good cricket brain: he captains the side well and he is a real competitor. In the slips or batting, he always gives 100 per cent – and his bowling is an art. Quick bowling tests your reflexes, but slow bowling tests you mentally. You can go into a 'zone' with quick bowling, but when you're facing Shane Warne you have to be fully switched on all the time. It's probably the biggest test you can have as a cricketer.

I would say that the best moments I've had in Test cricket have been when he is bowling and he's in your face and chirping you. I enjoy playing against him because I used to bowl a bit of leg spin myself – though obviously not in the same class – and I'm fairly at home against spin. But because he drifts the ball into you, like that ball to Gatting, your natural tendency is to just lean on it and push it to leg. That's what I did at Edgbaston when I was on 207 … and nicked it to Healy. That one-second lapse of concentration. That's when he'll get you. That's why he's constantly chirping you, to make you lose your concentration.

We've had a few run-ins, notably in the Carlton & United Series final at Sydney in February 1999, where we exchanged a few words. People said I lost my rag with him, but I didn't do anything different in that innings to any other. If he gives me stick, I'll give it back. So we had a few words and then about 10 overs later he brought himself back on and I ran down the wicket and got stumped. It's easy for people to put the two things together and say that mentally he did me, but if that was the case, I wouldn't have batted so long against him at Edgbaston.

But going back to 'That Ball', part of the magic came from Allan Border's sense of timing. As a captain, you know that it's important that your spinner comes on after the fall of a wicket, because it's easier playing spin once you've played yourself in. You need to be relaxed to play it well. That's why some players prefer to open the batting, because if they come in in the middle order with hard hands and tense arms, they can struggle against spin.

So Border saw Gatting come in and thought: "Now's a good time." But not even the great AB can have imagined just how dramatic it would be.

NASSER HUSSAIN'S ANALYSIS

'When you're facing Shane Warne you have to be fully switched on all the time. It's probably the biggest test you can have as a cricketer.'

Allan Border with the Ashes which he won as captain for the third time in 1993 by beating England 4-1

GEOFFREY BOYCOTT
V
MICHAEL HOLDING

MICHAEL HOLDING

GEOFFREY BOYCOTT

'That Over'

Third Test · Barbados · March 14, 1981

Michael Holding was known as Whispering Death, because you couldn't hear him coming.
As Geoffrey Boycott discovered, it was equally hard to see the balls he bowled,
let alone lay a bat on them…

> *'Holding bowled one of the fastest overs in the history of cricket; his last ball plucked out my off stump and sent it cartwheeling twenty yards. A strange silence settled briefly before pandemonium broke loose with thousands of people jumping up and down.'*
>
> GEOFFREY BOYCOTT,
> 'BOYCOTT ON CRICKET'

It was an eventful tour. But even amongst the tales of a deportation order, a cancelled Test match and a death in the party, one brief moment of cricket – one over, in fact – has achieved a place in the game's history.

England, under the captaincy of Ian Botham, were touring the West Indies for the first time for seven years.

They had lost the First Test in Trinidad by an innings and had also lost their vice-captain, Bob Willis, there. He had broken down and returned home to be replaced by Surrey's bustling fast-medium pace bowler, Robin Jackman.

Jackman had spent a large part of several British winters playing cricket in South Africa and, soon after his

THE PROTAGONISTS

Geoffrey Boycott
(Yorkshire & England)
Aged 40. Playing his
96th Test, having scored
7,215 runs. Had scored
120 first-class
hundreds. England's
third-highest run-scorer
with 8,114.

Michael Holding
(Jamaica & West Indies)
Aged 27. Playing his
26th Test and starting
with 101 wickets.
Bowling very fast
and with graceful
athleticism, he finished
his career with
249 wickets.

'Cool runnings, Mikey!'
Famous Bridgetown
spectator King Dial
(below) evidently
approves of Holding's
awesome power

arrival in Guyana, that contact with the home of apartheid was raised in a newspaper at the other end of the Caribbean. The deportation order that followed led to the cancellation of the Second Test and the whole team's departure from Georgetown for Barbados. In that island the foreign ministers of the countries on England's

'Aye, and if we get them out for 150, how many do you think we'll get?'

GEOFF BOYCOTT
BEFORE STARTING THE
ENGLAND INNINGS

Gooch is bowled by Joel Garner for 26, but made a century in the second innings. Right: Boycott – hot, bothered and bemused

itinerary met to decide the fate of the tour. After a week of uncertainty, the go-ahead was finally given, and a month after the First Test the Third began at Kensington Oval with Jackman in the England side to make his Test debut.

The pitch showed a lot more green than usual, so Botham put the West Indies in. Jackman's extraordinary week continued. Coming on as first change, he took the wicket of Gordon Greenidge in his first over and three

wickets on his first day in Test cricket. From 65 for 4, though, the West Indies got away, thanks to a century from Clive Lloyd, ably supported by Larry Gomes. Still, England were not too disappointed to have bowled them out for 265 early on the second day.

Jackman recalls the words of Geoff Boycott in the field on the first day when the new bowler was excited at seeing the West Indies in some trouble: "Aye, and if we get them out for 150, how many do you think we'll get on this?"

So the doubt had been put in the mind of the opening batsman, who had usually enjoyed success on this pitch.

The second day was not too far advanced when Graham Gooch and Boycott went out to open England's first innings. Gooch faced the first over from Andy Roberts and took six runs off it.

Sharing the new ball with Roberts was the athletic figure of Michael Holding. The loose-limbed Jamaican was marking a very long run-up out at the northern end, almost from the verandah of the green-roofed Pickwick Pavilion. Then, accelerating with deceptive grace towards the stumps, he was on his way.

Boycott would have expected it to be fast, but he might also have expected that his much-practised technique would enable him to play it. It was lightning fast, lifting from just short of a length and finding enough movement to beat the outside edge.

Nor did the speed relent for the next four balls. Two of them took him on the glove. Another nipped in to take him on the hip – painfully avoiding the thigh pad.

The great technician was being given a thorough examination. Each of the first five balls of the over had beaten him comprehensively.

Opinions vary about whether he even saw the sixth ball. It was full length and very fast indeed. Boycott may well have been in a bemused state of mind by this point, after his shattering experience thus far. He was not in line

and the ball plucked out his off stump and sent it a very long way back. Excitement in the crowd bubbled over. Some spectators rushed on to shake the Jamaican by the hand. Boycott bowled Holding 0.

Holding bowled ten more overs in the innings, took two more wickets and finished with three for 16. One of those wickets was Botham, caught behind for the equal top score of 26. He, too, shook his head at the sheer pace and

apologised to the England coach, Ken Barrington, that he really could not play against that. There was great poignancy in that. As Barrington watched the England for whom he himself had battled so hard in his time dismissed for 122, he was watching his last day's cricket. That night at the team hotel, Ken Barrington died of a heart attack.

He would have been proud of the way his team, who were all so fond of him, stuck to their task next day. But

Boycott peers into the distance, looking for his missing off stump. Viv Richards and Desmond Haynes join the crowd in blowing the roof off the Kensington Oval

West Indies v England

Kensington Oval, Bridgetown, Barbados
England won the toss and fielded

13.3.1981 - 18.3.1981
West Indies won by 298 runs

West Indies	1st innings		2nd innings	
C.G.Greenidge	c Gooch b Jackman	14	lbw b Dilley	0
D.L.Haynes	c Bairstow b Jackman	25	lbw b Botham	25
I.V.A.Richards	c Botham b Dilley	0	(4) not out	182
E.H.Mattis	lbw b Botham	16	(5) c Butcher b Jackman	24
*C.H.Lloyd	c Gooch b Jackman	100	(7) lbw b Botham	66
H.A.Gomes	c Botham b Dilley	58	run out	34
+D.A.Murray	c Bairstow b Dilley	9	(9) not out	5
A.M.E.Roberts	c Bairstow b Botham	14	c Bairstow b Botham	0
J.Garner	c Bairstow b Botham	15		
M.A.Holding	c Gatting b Botham	0		
C.E.H.Croft	not out	0	(3) c Boycott b Jackman	33
Extras	(b-4, lb-6, w-2, nb-2)	14	(b-3, lb-7, w-0, nb-0)	10
TOTAL	(all out)	265	(for 7 wickets declared)	379

Fall of Wickets	1-24	2-25	3-47	4-65	5-219		1-0	2-57	3-71	4-130	5-212
	6-224	7-236	8-258	9-258	10-265		6-365	7-365			

Bowling Analysis	O	M	R	W		O	M	R	W
G.R.Dilley	23	7	51	3		25	3	111	1
I.T.Botham	25.1	5	77	4		29	5	102	3
R.D.Jackman	22	4	65	3		25	5	76	2
J.E.Emburey	18	4	45	0		24	7	57	0
G.A.Gooch	2	0	13	0					
P.Willey	6	0	23	0					

England	1st innings		2nd innings	
G.A.Gooch	b Garner	26	c Garner b Croft	116
G.Boycott	b Holding	0	c Garner b Holding	1
M.W.Gatting	c Greenidge b Roberts	2	b Holding	0
D.I.Gower	c Mattis b Croft	17	b Richards	54
R.O.Butcher	c Richards b Croft	17	lbw b Richards	2
*I.T.Botham	c Murray b Holding	26	c Lloyd b Roberts	1
P.Willey	not out	19	lbw b Croft	17
+D.L.Bairstow	c Mattis b Holding	0	c Murray b Croft	2
J.E.Emburey	c Lloyd b Roberts	0	b Garner	9
R.D.Jackman	c Roberts b Croft	7	b Garner	7
G.R.Dilley	c Gomes b Croft	0	not out	7
Extras	(b-1, lb-1, w-0, nb-6)	8	(b-1, lb-3, w-0, nb-4)	8
TOTAL	(all out)	122	(all out)	224

Fall of Wickets	1-6	2-11	3-40	4-55	5-72		1-2	2-2	3-122	4-134	5-139
	6-94	7-94	8-97	9-122	10-122		6-196	7-198	8-201	9-213	10-224

Bowling Analysis	O	M	R	W		O	M	R	W
A.M.E.Roberts	11	3	29	2		20	6	42	1
M.A.Holding	11	7	16	3		19	6	46	2
C.E.H.Croft	13.5	5	39	4		19	1	65	3
J.Garner	12	5	30	1		16.2	6	39	2
I.V.A.Richards	17	6	24	2					

Umpires: D.M.Archer, D.Sang Hue

Much-loved Ken Barrington, who died of a heart attack that night

Viv Richards made a big hundred and England were set a notional 523 to win. Gooch made a century and Gower fifty, but England were beaten by 298 runs.

This time Michael Holding's first over had been even more successful. His fifth ball was a lifter to Boycott, to have him caught in the gully for 1. The next kept low to bowl Gatting first ball. Holding's match figures were 5 for 62. Boycott's were one run for twice out – to Holding.

NASSER HUSSAIN'S ANALYSIS

'Boycs might be a pain in the neck but he's the wicket we want'

Every England batsman of the past 30 years owes Michael Holding a drink, because whenever Boycs gets too overbearing, all you have to do is mention That Over. I've seen Ian Botham do it a few times, just to remind Geoffrey that he's human like the rest of us.

Whatever people may say about Boycs, the West Indies viewed him in the same way that the South Africans view Michael Atherton now: "He might be a pain in the neck but he's the wicket we want. He plays quick bowling pretty well and he's got a bit of guts and Northern grit about him … and if we get his wicket, the rest will come easily."

We've all seen his stump going cartwheeling, but the reason it was such a famous event was because it was the start of a new era for quick bowling. I think Geoffrey would be quite proud of it in a way. Even in 50 years' time, he can put the video in front of any batsman and challenge them to play that over. We say now that the bowlers are quicker than ever before, but I don't think anyone can argue that that was about as great as quick bowling gets.

It was on a decent Test wicket in Barbados – there was nothing suspect about the pitch, and certainly nothing suspect about the bowler's action. It was just a demonstration of the art of fast bowling. Holding seemed to get better and better with every ball.

Geoffrey's coaching ability is second to none – the way he talks about the mental side of batting, the preparation and how to play quick bowling. Even Graham Gooch used to hang on every word.

He's good, but he doesn't half like to let you know it. I remember Jimmy Whitaker at an England training session querying the fact that Boycott's suggested method of playing quick bowling was pure survival and scoring mainly in singles. Whitaker said: "What about Allan Lamb – he's got six hundreds against the West Indies because he takes them on." The next day Boycott brought in a copy of *Wisden* – simply to prove that his record against the West Indies was better than Lamb's. (Boycott averaged 45.94 to Lamb's 34.41, though only one of Boycott's five hundreds was after 1974.)

So, as I say, we all owe Michael Holding a drink. Imagine how insufferable Geoffrey would be if it hadn't been for That Over!

'We've all seen his stump going cartwheeling, but the reason it was such a famous event was because it was the start of a new era for quick bowling.'

Warriors' pride

KAPIL DEV V HEMMINGS · LORD'S · 1990

TENDULKAR V AUSTRALIA · PERTH · 1992

LARA V AUSTRALIA · WEST INDIES · 1999

SOUTH AFRICA V WALSH & AMBROSE · BARBADOS · 1992

GOOCH V AMBROSE · HEADINGLEY · 1991

Opposite: Clenched-fist salutes for Curtly Ambrose and Courtney Walsh after defeating South Africa
This page: Kapil Dev, Sachin Tendulkar, a banner at Barbados, Curtly Ambrose, and Graham Gooch

CRICKET'S GREATEST BATTLES

KAPIL DEV
V
EDDIE HEMMINGS

KAPIL DEV

EDDIE HEMMINGS

'I'll get 'em in sixes'

Second Test • Lord's • June 30, 1990

*Having scored 333, Graham Gooch probably thought he was on a roll.
So when India needed 24 to save the follow-on with one wicket to fall, he cunningly invited
Eddie Hemmings to lay a trap for Kapil Dev. What happened next wasn't in Gooch's script*

*Opposite: Russell and
Hemmings can only
watch helplessly as
Kapil Dev hits his
fourth six in four balls
to save the follow-on*

This was a Test match with so much to applaud, though few, probably not even the perpetrator himself, applauded Mohammed Azharuddin's decision to put England in to bat when he won the toss for India. England – and particularly their captain, Graham Gooch – took full toll, though Azharuddin was later to make some

amends with some glorious batting of his own. And then came the outrageous audacity of the remarkable Kapil Dev.

Kapil had enjoyed India's only success of the first morning of the Test, bowling Mike Atherton. But Gooch and David Gower put on 127 together and by the end of the first day Gooch was six short of 200, Allan Lamb had

*Anything you can do…
Graham Gooch hits a six
in his innings of 333,
which brought Lord's to
its feet (opposite).
Below: India captain
Mohammed Azharuddin
scored a century in just
88 balls. Earlier, when he
put England in to bat, he
could not have foreseen
the amazing scoreboard
at the end of the innings*

104 and poor Azharuddin was already being pilloried for his decision. He was made to suffer more next day as the third-wicket stand rose to 308. Even when Lamb went for 139, Gooch was joined by Robin Smith in another substantial partnership.

Gooch was finally bowled by Manoj Prabhakar for 333, just when Sir Len Hutton, looking on, must have been expecting to see his celebrated 364 overhauled. When Smith got his 100, England declared at 653 for 4.

There was still an hour to go on the second day and India faced a target of 454 just to avoid the follow-on. Opening the innings, Ravi Shastri replied with a century, but then came the star of the day – Azharuddin. Early on

TOTAL		
Nº6	653	Nº5
4 Wkts	4	100
	LAST WKT	641
LAST MAN 333 B		B 9
10 BOWLER 9 OVERS		71

he tucked into one over of Hemmings' off spin with four wristy boundaries. He reached his hundred off 88 balls and a large Saturday crowd cheered him to the echo.

India entered the fourth day needing another 78 runs to avoid the follow-on. Azharuddin was on 117 and with him was the mercurial Kapil Dev, so the odds, even with six wickets down, looked good. But then Hemmings bowled Azharuddin for 121. Seven wickets down and the follow-on target still 61 runs away. Kiran More stayed with Kapil while that was reduced by 37, but when Angus Fraser dismissed More and Yashpal Sharma in the space of three balls India looked doomed to bat again.

At 430 for 9, the last man coming in was the small, bespectacled Narendra Hirwani, a player whose skills lay in

Blood among the rhododendrons

KAPIL DEV V ZIMBABWE • 1983

Kapil's four-sixes-in-four-balls was by no means the first example of his devastating batting. In 1983 he played arguably the greatest World Cup innings ever, against Zimbabwe at Tunbridge Wells. Both teams had pulled off shock results in earlier games, India beating the West Indies while Zimbabwe had surprised Australia. Now they were vying to reach the semi-finals.

Kapil Dev won the toss and opted to bat. But Zimbabwe's seamers, Peter Rawson and Kevin Curran, soon had India in deep trouble at 9 for 4.

Enter Kapil Dev, the only possible saviour. But within three overs the crisis had worsened. Yashpal Sharma was caught behind off Rawson. India were 17 for 5 in the 13th over and their semi-final hopes were looking forlorn.

The Indian captain's first job was to stop the rot. Rawson and Curran could not bowl for ever. With Roger Binny he added 60 before Binny was LBW to John Traicos for 22, and in the next over Duncan Fletcher removed Shastri. India were deep in trouble once more at 78 for 7.

Kapil continued trying to eke out the innings until lunch came with India 106 for 7. After the interval, though, he decided to attack. He and Madan Lal added 69 in 16 overs, before Curran had Madan Lal caught behind.

At 140 for 8, India were still vulnerable, but Syed Kirmani came in looking

Cap'n Kapil at Tunbridge Wells

confident. Kapil promptly launched into the Zimbabwean attack, lobbing numerous missiles into the rhododendrons behind the short boundaries to reach 100 from only 72 balls.

Over the last ten overs of the innings, the Zimbabweans' tigerish fielding began to crumble. Kapil and Kirmani put on 126 – a world-record ninth-wicket stand for a one-day international. Kapil Dev's 174 not out, including six sixes and 17 fours, was then the highest score in any one-day international.

Zimbabwe fell 31 short of India's 226 for 8, and Kapil's team went on to achieve one of the biggest upsets in cricket history by beating the West Indies in the World Cup Final at Lord's. The turning point in that dramatic match came when the in-form Viv Richards fell to a spectacular running catch by – who else? – Kapil Dev.

his leg-spin bowling and not his batting. There was one ball of Fraser's over to go and 24 runs needed to save the follow-on that was likely to mean the difference between defeat and a draw. Hirwani survived, but Kapil Dev knew that in his hands alone lay India's salvation. Eddie Hemmings was to bowl to him from the Nursery End.

Behind Hemmings the Compton and Edrich Stands were under construction, so that end of the ground was inhabited only by builders and quantities of scaffolding poles. The straight boundary had been moved in a yard or two to accommodate this activity. England would settle now for Kapil taking a single early in the over to expose Hirwani, but he pushed the first two balls of Hemmings' over back defensively.

To the third ball, however, Kapil stepped down the pitch and drove Hemmings imperiously back over his head for six.

Food for thought for Hemmings. But if Kapil was going to try this approach, he might easily mis-hit. The next ball was tossed up invitingly and the Indian all-rounder took the bait – driving extravagantly again into the scaffolding behind Hemmings. Six more.

Twelve were needed now to avoid the follow-on. Two balls were left in the over. The field came in a bit. They did

'Well, here's the last ball of the over. Hemmings bowls it. Kapil Dev is going for the big hit. It's going to do it, is it? He's done it! He's saved the follow-on. He's broken a world record. He shakes his fist to the Indian dressing room and if that isn't one of the most remarkable things you've ever seen in cricket, I don't know what is...'

CHRISTOPHER
MARTIN-JENKINS,
COMMENTATING FOR
'TEST MATCH SPECIAL'

Walking into the record books: Kapil Dev smites Eddie Hemmings for six at Lord's

not want Kapil stealing a single to take the strike. Nothing was further from his mind as he advanced again – and Hemmings almost cricked his neck as the ball sailed above him and over the builders' screens for a third successive six.

What glorious stuff. Six runs away from the follow-on target. Now, where was he going to push the single to get down the other end for Fraser's next over?

He wasn't. Unbelievably, gloriously and in the true swashbuckling mode of the dashing heroes of the prolific Indian film industry's epics, Kapil Dev did it again. His fourth six was probably the biggest of the four, landing well back among the rubble of the half-completed stand.

Kapil nonchalantly watched it go with the air of one who could not see anything particularly remarkable about it. But Indians in the crowd danced in celebration. In four blows he had ensured that England would have to bat again and had given India a very good chance of drawing the Test match. Off the first ball of the next over, Hirwani was LBW

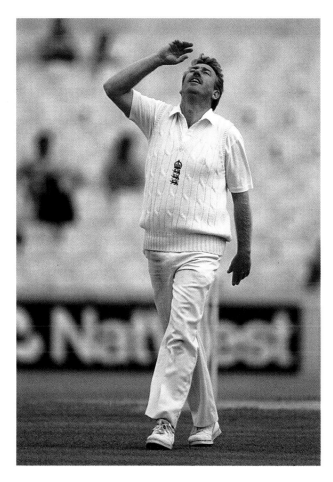

Eddie didn't know whether to laugh or cry ... but had the last laugh

to Fraser and India were all out for 454 – 199 runs behind.

They found themselves batting again that evening, after Gooch had crashed another century – 123 from 113 balls, putting on 204 for the first wicket and making it possible to declare shortly before the close, leaving a target of 454. Both openers were gone before the end of the fourth day and at lunch on the final day India were 158 for 6.

Shortly after the interval came a moment of sweet revenge. Kapil Dev pulled a ball from Eddie Hemmings. It hung in the air before landing in the safe hands of Chris Lewis at midwicket. Hemmings had got his tormentor.

There was no way out for India now. They succumbed in mid-afternoon – bowled out for 224. England had won by 247 runs.

England v India

Lord's, London, England
India won the toss and fielded

26.7.1990 - 31.7.1990
England won by 247 runs

England	1st innings		2nd innings	
*G.A.Gooch	b Prabhakar	333	c Azharuddin b Sharma	123
M.A.Atherton	b Kapil Dev	8	c Vengsarkar b Sharma	72
D.I.Gower	c Manjrekar b Hirwani	40	not out	32
A.J.Lamb	c Manjrekar b Sharma	139	c Tendulkar b Hirwani	19
R.A.Smith	not out	100	b Prabhakar	15
J.E.Morris	not out	4		
+R.C.Russell				
C.C.Lewis				
E.E.Hemmings				
A.R.C.Fraser				
D.E.Malcolm				
Extras	(b-2, lb-21, w-2, nb-4)	29	(b-0, lb-11, w-0, nb-0)	11
TOTAL	(for 4 wickets declared)	**653**	(for 4 wickets declared)	**272**

Fall of Wickets	1-14	2-141	3-449	4-641	1-204	2-207	3-250	4-272

Bowling Analysis	O	M	R	W	O	M	R	W
Kapil Dev	34	5	120	1	10	0	53	0
M.Prabhakar	43	6	187	1	11.2	2	45	1
S.K.Sharma	33	5	122	1	15	0	75	2
R.J.Shastri	22	0	99	0	7	0	38	0
N.D.Hirwani	30	1	102	1	11	0	50	1

India	1st innings		2nd innings	
R.J.Shastri	c Gooch b Hemmings	100	c Russell b Malcolm	12
N.S.Sidhu	c Morris b Fraser	30	c Morris b Fraser	1
S.V.Manjrekar	c Russell b Gooch	18	c Russell b Malcolm	33
D.B.Vengsarkar	c Russell b Fraser	52	c Russell b Hemmings	35
*M.Azharuddin	b Hemmings	121	c Atherton b Lewis	37
S.R.Tendulkar	b Lewis	10	c Gooch b Fraser	27
M.Prabhakar	c Lewis b Malcolm	25	lbw b Lewis	8
Kapil Dev	not out	77	c Lewis b Hemmings	7
+K.S.More	c Morris b Fraser	8	lbw b Fraser	16
S.K.Sharma	c Russell b Fraser	0	run out	38
N.D.Hirwani	lbw b Fraser	0	not out	0
Extras	(b-0, lb-1, w-4, nb-8)	13	(b-3, lb-1, w-0, nb-6)	10
TOTAL	(all out)	**454**	(all out)	**224**

Fall of Wickets	1-63	2-102	3-191	4-241	5-288	1-9	2-23	3-63	4-114	5-127
	6-348	7-393	8-430	9-430	10-454	6-140	7-158	8-181	9-206	10-224

Bowling Analysis	O	M	R	W	O	M	R	W
D.E.Malcolm	25	1	106	1	10	0	65	2
A.R.C.Fraser	39.1	9	104	5	22	7	39	3
C.C.Lewis	24	3	108	1	8	1	26	2
G.A.Gooch	6	3	26	1				
E.E.Hemmings	20	3	109	2	21	2	79	2
M.A.Atherton	1	0	11	0				

Umpires: H.D.Bird, N.T.Plews   **Man of the Match:** G.A.Gooch

NASSER HUSSAIN'S ANALYSIS

'All credit to Kapil Dev for calling Graham Gooch's bluff'

'It was Gooch's decision to have Eddie Hemmings on at that time... Personally I would have been bowling two quicks at Hirwani.'

Perhaps this battle ought to be Kapil Dev versus Graham Gooch, because Gooch was the England captain, and it was his decision to have Eddie Hemmings on at that time. Maybe Gooch just wanted another bat – after all, he wouldn't have got that second-innings century if India had followed on. As for Kapil Dev, well, Gooch had scored 333 and India's opening bowler obviously couldn't wait to have another bowl at him.

Seriously, though, all credit to Kapil Dev for calling Graham Gooch's bluff: the Indian all-rounder pressed G for gamble and it came off.

Knowing that Kapil liked to hit in the air, Gooch decided to lay down the challenge: "The only way you're going to get past the follow-on is to hit Eddie for four sixes.

'It was unbelievable stuff. He launched a counter-attack the like of which one had never seen before. We were applauding each and every shot. Our hands became weary but each shot was absolutely thrilling.'
SUNIL GAVASKAR
ON KAPIL'S WORLD CUP INNINGS VERSUS ZIMBABWE

We'll put two men back, and have a go if you want to." He did have a go. Four times. And hit them all for six.

Personally I would have been bowling two quicks at Hirwani, because if Kapil had wanted to take a single, he wouldn't have dared to do it if it had meant exposing Hirwani to a fast bowler.

And Kapil would never have scored four sixes off a fast bowler – the only time I can remember a quick bowler being hit for even three sixes was when Andrew Flintoff did it to Alex Tudor, when he took 28 off an over at Old Trafford in 1998.

Kapil's record is amazing. Whichever table you look at – batting, bowling, Tests, one-dayers – he sneaks up there.

As a batsman he was lethal. Remember that amazing innings against Zimbabwe at Tunbridge Wells in the 1983

NASSER HUSSAIN'S ANALYSIS

'The Indian all-rounder pressed G for gamble and it came off.'

World Cup, when he came in at number six and scored 175 not out in a total of 266 for 8. It really was a one-man show. A few months before that he had scored the fastest ever Test fifty, in 30 balls against Pakistan.

This is a guy who also took 434 Test wickets – and don't forget where he did most of his bowling. These days the wickets in Asia are more conducive to pace, but in Kapil's day they were dead featherbeds for seam bowlers.

On top of that, he was captain of India when they won the World Cup. He certainly was some player.

'As a batsman he was lethal…' Kapil Dev at Lord's in 1990

CRICKET'S GREATEST BATTLES

SACHIN TENDULKAR
V
AUSTRALIA

'He plays very
much the same as
I played ... the
compactness, his
stroke production
and technique.'

DON BRADMAN
ON TENDULKAR

SACHIN TENDULKAR

AUSTRALIA'S CRAIG McDERMOTT

Going down with all guns blazing

Fifth Test · Perth · Febuary 2 & 3, 1992

*The Asians had raved about Sachin Tendulkar for years, but what could this tiny 18-year-old
do against a rip-roaring Australian pace attack on their favourite hunting ground at Perth?
With the Indians' ship listing ignominiously, the boy stood on the burning deck...*

I ndia had been taking a hammering. Australia had beaten them by a distance in the First Test in Brisbane and the Second in Melbourne. However, the visitors had bounced back in the Third Test, with a double century from Ravi Shastri and a substantial hundred from the teenager, Sachin Tendulkar, but rain in Sydney had prevented a result. In Adelaide Australia had won by 38 runs with ten wickets for McDermott – among them

WARRIORS' PRIDE

164

Sachin Tendulkar
(Bombay & India)
Aged 18. Playing his 16th Test, having played his first aged 16 – the third-youngest Test player ever. Had previously made 837 runs with two centuries.

Australia
Had become a formidable team over the previous four years under Allan Border, with a fast bowling attack spearheaded by Craig McDermott and Merv Hughes.

Azharuddin for the hundred that so nearly took India to victory. Now the Final Test was to be played out on the fastest pitch in Australia – the WACA ground in Perth.

David Boon's third consecutive Test century, supported by Allan Border's 59 and a rapid 50 by Tom Moody on his home ground, took Australia to a first-innings total of 346.

Now for India to face the steep Perth bounce and a new ball in the hands of Craig McDermott, who already had 28 wickets in the series, and Merv Hughes. Hughes it was who made the first breakthrough, having Navjot Sidhu caught behind for 5. Forty-four runs came for the second wicket before McDermott snapped up Kris Srikkanth for 34.

At 69 for 2, in came the diminutive 18-year-old, Sachin Tendulkar. The ball was lifting uncomfortably as it was fired in by the two big fast bowlers, McDermott and Hughes, and supporting their fierce aggression were two

And the centuries just keep on coming... Indian fans mob Tendulkar as he reaches three figures in Jo'burg later in 1992

more very useful seamers, Paul Reiffel and Mike Whitney.

In the face of this onslaught, Tendulkar started with obdurate tenacity. He and Sanjay Manjrekar saw the score to three figures before Hughes had Manjrekar for 31. The Indians' most senior batting came now, but Dilip Vengsarkar did not last long before Hughes had him caught at slip for 1. Mohammed Azharuddin, the captain, had made 11 when McDermott had him caught behind.

By the close of the second day, India were in considerable trouble at 135 for 5. Tendulkar was 31 not out.

The nightwatchman, Venkatapathy Raju, departed in the morning before a run had been added. Kapil Dev helped Tendulkar add 24, which passed the follow-on target, before he holed out to Whitney for 4 and Manoj Prabhakar did the same for a duck.

India were down and all but out at 159 for 8. Kiran

More, the wicketkeeper, was not without some pretensions as a batsman, but now Tendulkar decided to carry the attack to the Australian bowlers. With the Perth bounce favouring his savage cutting, he started to plunder the square cover boundary. The 200 came up, with Tendulkar starting to find gaps in the Australian field with surgical precision. He raced from 50 to his third Test century from only 55 balls, his defiance bringing what had seemed an all too one-sided contest to life. More proved the ideal foil as the youngster took the centre stage in their ninth-wicket stand of 81, setting a new Indian record.

Eventually it was Whitney who claimed Tendulkar – caught at slip for a brilliant 114, which had come from 161 balls and had held up Australia for three-and-three-quarter hours. He had hit 16 fours. More was inspired enough to continue, providing the lion's share of a last-wicket stand

Craig McDermott took 31 wickets in the series as Australia crushed India, but 18-year-old Sachin Tendulkar set out his stall with two centuries and a tour average of 46

'*He is sent from upstairs to play.*'

RAVI SHASTRI ON TENDULKAR WHEN HE WAS AGED 15

Australia v India

W.A.C.A., Perth, Australia
Australia won the toss and batted

1.2.1992 - 5.2.1992
Australia won by 300 runs

Australia	1st innings		2nd innings	
M.A.Taylor	c Srikkanth b Kapil Dev	2	(2) lbw b Kapil Dev	16
W.N.Phillips	c More b Prabhakar	8	(1) c Kapil Dev b Srinath	14
D.C.Boon	c Sidhu b Prabhakar	107	c Kapil Dev b Prabhakar	38
*A.R.Border	c Srikkanth b Kapil Dev	59	(8) not out	20
D.M.Jones	c Srikkanth b Raju	7	(4) not out	150
T.M.Moody	c Vengsarkar b Prabhakar	50	(5) c More b Kapil Dev	101
+I.A.Healy	c More b Srinath	28	(6) c More b Raju	7
M.G.Hughes	c Srikkanth b Srinath	24	(7) c Tendulkar b Srinath	11
P.R.Reiffel	c More b Prabhakar	9		
C.J.McDermott	c Srikkanth b Prabhakar	31		
M.R.Whitney	not out	1		
Extras	(b-1, lb-7, w-0, nb-12)	20	(b-0, lb-4, w-0, nb-6)	10
TOTAL	(all out)	**346**	(for 6 wickets declared)	**367**

Fall of Wickets	1-10	2-21	3-138	4-145	5-232		1-27	2-31	3-113	4-286	5-298
	6-259	7-290	8-303	9-338	10-346		6-315				

Bowling Analysis	O	M	R	W		O	M	R	W
Kapil Dev	40	12	103	2		28	8	48	2
M.Prabhakar	32.5	9	101	5		32	4	116	1
J.Srinath	25	5	69	2		29.3	3	121	2
S.R.Tendulkar	5	2	9	0					
Venkatapathy Raju	23	6	56	1		24	5	78	1

India	1st innings		2nd innings	
K.Srikkanth	c Boon b McDermott	34	(2) c Jones b Whitney	38
N.S.Sidhu	c Healy b Hughes	5	(1) c Jones b Reiffel	35
S.V.Manjrekar	c Jones b Hughes	31	c Healy b Whitney	8
S.R.Tendulkar	c Moody b Whitney	114	c Moody b Reiffel	5
D.B.Vengsarkar	c Taylor b Hughes	1	c Moody b Whitney	4
*M.Azharuddin	c Healy b McDermott	11	lbw b Whitney	24
Venkatapathy Raju	c Taylor b Whitney	1	(10) c Healy b Whitney	8
Kapil Dev	c Hughes b Whitney	4	(7) lbw b Whitney	0
M.Prabhakar	c Reiffel b Whitney	0	(8) c Healy b McDermott	3
+K.S.More	c Healy b Hughes	43	(9) c Taylor b Whitney	1
J.Srinath	not out	5	not out	1
Extras	(b-0, lb-14, w-0, nb-9)	23	(b-0, lb-11, w-0, nb-3)	14
TOTAL	(all out)	**272**	(all out)	**141**

Fall of Wickets	1-25	2-69	3-100	4-109	5-130		1-82	2-90	3-97	4-103	5-111
	6-135	7-159	8-159	9-240	10-272		6-111	7-126	8-129	9-134	10-141

Bowling Analysis	O	M	R	W		O	M	R	W
C.J.McDermott	21	6	47	2		20	8	44	1
M.G.Hughes	26.5	5	82	4		12	2	25	0
P.R.Reiffel	17	5	46	0		11	2	34	2
M.R.Whitney	23	4	68	4		12.1	3	27	7
T.M.Moody	2	0	15	0					

Umpires: A.R.Crafter, T.A.Prue   **Man of the Match:** M.R.Whitney

of 32 with Javagal Srinath, which took India to 272, 74 runs adrift, but much closer than had seemed likely earlier in the day. The last two wickets had added 113.

Kapil Dev and Srinath had sent back both the Australian openers before the lead had reached 150, keeping India's hopes alive. But then Moody made a powerful 101 while Dean Jones battled his way into form to reach 150 before Border declared, setting a notional target of 442.

India's best start of the series took them well into the final morning's play before a wicket fell, but then it precipitated a procession. And this time Tendulkar was amongst them, as Mike Whitney enjoyed his finest hour, taking 7 for 27 and dismissing India for 141.

Australia won by a massive 300 runs and took the series 4-0. But, for all the runs of Boon, Jones, Moody and the rest, Australians knew that in the 18-year-old Sachin Tendulkar they had seen a new star.

NASSER HUSSAIN'S ANALYSIS

'This was the innings that made the world stand up and take notice'

'Tendulkar has always been positive against Shane Warne and has tried to hit him out of the attack, and more often than not he has succeeded.'

The Indian players aren't used to bouncy wickets. They have the same problem we do, in that their home pitches are very much of one type, so when they go to Australia or the West Indies, they don't have the right batting experience. Recently, people like Saurav Ganguly and Rahul Dravid have gone to Australia with a Test average of 50 and have rather been found out, although they're very good players. Sachin Tendulkar is the only one who has immediately adapted to extremely foreign conditions, even when he was young.

The amazing thing about this performance is that he had probably never played on a wicket like Perth, apart from a brief sighter earlier in the tour. After you've played there a few times, you learn that, because of the bounce, you can leave balls you wouldn't leave in England

and you can pull balls off a length. But Tendulkar went there as an 18-year-old after playing schoolboy cricket on a low, slow spinners' wicket in Bombay, and immediately scored a century.

They already knew all about him in India, of course, and he had scored his first Test century in England in 1990. But this was the innings that made the world stand up and take notice, since it was against the might of Australia. To go there after such a huge build-up and still score runs was phenomenal.

There was an unbelievable weight of expectation on him in Asia, and he really has lived up to it. The way he has carried himself is exceptional. In India in 1998, Shane Warne was Australia's biggest threat, but Tendulkar has always been positive against him and has tried to hit him out of the attack, and more often than not he has succeeded. In Australia's first

NASSER HUSSAIN'S ANALYSIS

'There was an unbelievable weight of expectation on him in Asia, and he really has lived up to it.'

Cricket's number one pin-up at work, rest and play: 'Although he's a millionaire now, the Yorkshire lads say he's still very down-to-earth…'

game of that tour, Tendulkar scored 204 not out against Warne. A fortnight later in the First Test he took him for an undefeated 155 and in the Third he hit 177 to finish with an average of 150 against Warne on that tour.

The Australians pay Tendulkar the ultimate compliment of comparing him to Bradman, as Bradman does himself. Bowlers say he has everything. Time and again Tendulkar stamps his authority on the game. When Graham Gooch was at his peak, he was both

technically brilliant and had the destructive power to demolish any attack. But Tendulkar has been like that throughout his career.

Although he's a millionaire now, the Yorkshire lads say he's still very down-to-earth. The last time I saw him was in an Indian restaurant in Birmingham. Ninety per cent of the people in there were saying, "Oh look, there's Tendulkar," while about two were saying: "There's Nasser Hussain" – and they were the ones I'd come in with.

BRIAN LARA
V
AUSTRALIA

THE PROTAGONISTS

Brian Lara
(Trinidad & West Indies)
Aged 29. Playing his
62nd Test. Appointed
captain of West Indies
in 1998. Holder of the
world record score
in both Tests (375)
and first-class cricket
(501 n.o.).

Australia
Fresh from defeating
England in Australia
3-1, hailed as unofficial
world Test champions.
Attack included two of
the best bowlers in the
world in fast bowler
Glenn McGrath and
legendary leg spinner
Shane Warne.

BRIAN LARA

AUSTRALIA

The resurrection of Brian

Third Test · Barbados · March 30, 1999

*Everyone knew that Brian Lara could flay ordinary attacks for record-breaking scores.
But the cares of office had weighed him down, his team and his own form were in rapid decline,
and as he prepared to face the world champions, he seemed like a broken man...*

It was the end of a thoroughly demoralising season for the West Indies. After a threatened players' strike over payments for their tour to South Africa, they had lost the Test series there 5-0 and gone down 6-1 in the one-day series. Licking their wounds in their own islands, a visit from Australia was hardly the ideal way to recuperate. The selectors did not give their captain, Brian Lara, a ringing endorsement, appointing him only for the first two Tests. And the series started as badly as could be anticipated.

In Trinidad, left 364 to win, the West Indies were bowled out for their lowest-ever score of 51 by Glenn McGrath and Jason Gillespie. Six successive Test

Despair and triumph for Brian Lara as he is run out in the First Test for 62 and the West Indies crash to defeat (above), but then hits a double century in Jamaica to take his team to a ten-wicket victory

defeats – each one, it seemed, more humiliating than the last.

The apparent lack of heart was being much derided up and down the Caribbean. But then Lara, possibly at the last gasp of his tenure of office, took the Second Test in Jamaica by the scruff of the neck. Rescuing the West Indies from 34 for 4 in reply to Australia's 256, he made 213, sharing a fifth-wicket stand of 344 with Jimmy Adams. The West Indies totalled 431, and then the off spinner Nehemiah Perry, playing in his first Test, took five wickets to set up a series-levelling win by ten wickets.

In Barbados it seemed that normal service had resumed. Steve Waugh, after winning the toss, made 199 and shared a stand of 281 with Ricky Ponting, who made 104. Australia ran up 490 and then McGrath and Gillespie soon got among the West Indian batting again.

Eight wickets were down, including the heroic Sherwin Campbell for 105, before the follow-on was saved and the eventual deficit was 161.

Perhaps Australia became complacent. Wickets tumbled – five to the indefatigable Courtney Walsh – and only some late hitting out by Warne took the total to 146. Suddenly, the West Indies had a chance ... but they would need 308 in four sessions of play.

Sherwin Campbell and Adrian Griffith gave them an ideal start on that fourth evening, putting on 72 for the first wicket, before three LBWs, while six runs were added, plunged the West Indies into the mire. Brian Lara was in before the close at 85 for 3. The remaining 223 needed for victory seemed a very long way off.

Lara started the final day with two runs to his name. Griffith was 35, but did not add to that before Gillespie had him LBW. It looked a hopeless situation at 91 for 4.

Gillespie and McGrath were scenting the kill and making scoring difficult even for Lara, who needed 47 balls to get into double figures. Carl Hooper was capable

of the sort of innings that seemed to be required, but today he edged Gillespie to Ian Healy behind the wicket to be out for 6. It was 105 for 5 and the writing was surely on the wall as Jimmy Adams came in to join his captain.

After a gruelling hour of testing examination from the two fast bowlers, McGrath and Gillespie were rested and the two leg spinners introduced. That move seemed to throw a switch in Lara. Shane Warne was pulled for six on to the roof of the stand at midwicket and Stuart MacGill despatched for three boundaries in an over.

McGrath may have been hoping to graze in the deep field until lunch, but he had to be brought back to try to curb such liberties. His burden was increased by a back strain suffered by Gillespie, but he found the fire to clang Lara on the helmet with a bouncer and could not resist following it up with several words, which sparked an exchange that required Adams' calming influence to defuse it. Lara had the last laugh, pulling the main Australian spearhead for four.

At lunch they had reached 161 for 5, with Adams the ideal foil, as the sixth-wicket stand stretched into the afternoon session and Lara cut loose, going from 50 to 100 in 51 balls and bringing up three figures with a lofted on-drive for four off Warne. It was an innings sometimes of savage power and sometimes of the most delicate and exquisite timing. But soon after Lara had reached his hundred, the toiling McGrath produced a beauty to nip back into the left-handed Adams and bowl him for 38. That was his contribution to the stand of 133, but most importantly he had stayed with Lara and, at 238 for 6, they had pulled the West Indies right back into the match.

Now only 70 more runs were needed, but they looked a long way off as McGrath quickly had both Ridley Jacobs and Perry LBW. At 248 for 8, the last two wickets needed to raise 60. But one of them was Lara. Curtly Ambrose

Glenn McGrath gives Brian Lara a few words of advice after having hit the batsman on the head with a bouncer

West Indies v Australia

Four-match Test series   West Indies 1999

1st Test – Trinidad   5.3.1999 - 8.3.1999
Australia won by 312 runs

Australia 1st innings	269 all out
G.S.Blewett 58	C.E.L.Ambrose 3-35

West indies 1st innings	167 all out
B.C.Lara 62	G.D.McGrath 5-50
D.R.E.Joseph 50	

Australia 2nd innings	261 all out
M.J.Slater 106	C.A.Walsh 4-67

West Indies 2nd innings 51 all out	
R.D.Jacobs 19	G.D.McGrath 5-28
B.C.Lara 3	J.N.Gillespie 4-18

2nd Test – Jamaica   13.3.1999 - 16.3.1999
West Indies won by 10 wickets

Australia 1st innings	266 all out
S.R.Waugh 100	C.A.Walsh 4-55
M.E.Waugh 67	

West Indies 1st innings	431 all out
B.C.Lara 213	G.D.McGrath 5-93
J.C.Adams 94	

Australia 2nd innings	177 all out
G.S.Blewett 30	N.O.Perry 5-70

West Indies 2nd innings 3-0

3rd Test – Barbados   26.3.1999 - 30.3.1999
West Indies won by 1 wicket

Australia 1st innings	490 all out
S.R.Waugh 199	N.O.Perry 3-102
R.T.Ponting 104	
J.L.Langer 51	

West Indies 1st innings	329 all out
S.L.Campbell 105	G.D.McGrath 4-128
R.D.Jacobs 68	
B.C.Lara 8	

Australia 2nd innings	146 all out
S.K.Warne 32	C.A.Walsh 5-39

West Indies 2nd innings 311-9	
B.C.Lara 153 not out	G.D.McGrath 5-92

4th Test – Antigua   3.4.1999 - 7.4.1999
Australia won by 176 runs

Australia 1st innings	303 all out
S.R.Waugh 72 not out	C.E.L.Ambrose 5-94
J.L.Langer 51	

West Indies 1st innings	222 all out
B.C.Lara 100	G.D.McGrath 3-64

Australia 2nd innings	306 all out
J.L.Langer 127	C.A.Walsh 4-78
M.E.Waugh 65	

West Indies 2nd innings 211 all out	
A.F.G.Griffith 56	G.D.McGrath 3-50
B.C.Lara 7	

was with him, unorthodoxly holding up an end for an hour and twenty minutes. By now only seven more were wanted. Crucially, Gillespie returned to the attack and with extra speed and a little movement found the edge of Lara's bat. Healy dived left, in front of first slip, got a glove on it – and incredibly dropped the chance.

But Gillespie, despite that exasperation, had another shot in his locker. An edge from Ambrose was clung onto by Elliott at third slip. It was 302 for 9.

Only six runs were needed, but the best friends of Courtney Walsh, now coming out, would not normally put him among the world's top batsmen. Soon he was berating himself for nibbling at a ball outside his off stump, but he had not made contact. Gillespie bowled a no-ball. The exhausted McGrath, now past his 40th over in sapping heat, bowled a wide. Four more needed.

At last a single down to fine leg for Lara brought the scores level. Off the first ball of the next over he opened his shoulders to drive Gillespie through the covers for four, bringing up his 150 and winning a remarkable match by one wicket. In the space of two Tests Lara had gone from villain to hero with two incredible solo efforts.

Steve Waugh reckoned in the aftermath that it was the best Test match he had played in. He could afford to be magnanimous a week later when, despite yet another hundred for Lara, a win in the Fourth and final Test in Antigua helped Australia to tie the series and therefore retain the Frank Worrell Trophy.

Left: A moment to match any of his record-breaking feats – Brian Lara grabs a souvenir after leading the West Indies to a dramatic victory by one wicket in Barbados

NASSER HUSSAIN'S ANALYSIS

'It was the last chance saloon. The question was how would Lara respond?'

Right: Brian Lara is hugged by supporters and then disappears into a sea of celebration as his 153 not out clinches a cliffhanger Test match in Barbados

What distinguished Lara's performances on this tour was the pressure he was under. His team had lost 5-0 in South Africa. People were saying they were on the skids and he wasn't interested. I've heard that when he tossed the coin before the Second Test in Jamaica, he said to Steve Waugh: "This is the last time I'll be doing this for a while."

So it was the last chance saloon. The question was how would Lara respond? If he was mentally weak, he could take the view that he had established himself as a great player, and from now on he would be content with playing for the West Indies and making a decent contribution. If he was mentally strong, he would take the responsibility and show he was still the best player not just in the West Indies but in the world.

I first got to know Lara when we played together in the Youth World Cup in Australia, and even then he was a very fluent, classical player who you would pay money to go and watch. But now he had to prove that he could still do it when the going got tough.

I was actually commenting on that tour for Sky TV – I went in like a sad case and sat in the studio with Charles Colville – and I watched in admiration as Lara completely turned things round. The West Indies had been humiliated in the First Test, and in Jamaica they were deep in trouble again. But when Lara came in it was noticeable that he had a different look in his eye. I remember saying that he seemed very focused. He wasn't flashing outside leg stump, and was obviously determined to play a long innings. He was in his

NASSER HUSSAIN'S ANALYSIS

'They had been praying for something from their little prince, Lara, and he came up with more than anyone could have expected. Sheer genius.'

zone. Something clicked for him that day that led him to produce those two games which he won virtually singlehandedly.

It was the classic example of one man taking on the opposition. The West Indies' batting was a shambles. The old guard had gone; the new people weren't working out. Australia knew they only had to get him out and they'd win the game. But on two occasions, not only did they not get him out, but he scored 213 and 153 not out.

'When Lara came in it was noticeable that he had a different look in his eye.'

Remember the people running on the pitch in celebration. You can understand why, especially in West Indies cricket where there is so much pride. They had been praying for something from their little prince, Lara, and he came up with more than anyone could have expected. Sheer genius.

That's why those three stand above the rest in modern cricket. Brian Lara, Steve Waugh and Sachin Tendulkar. They regularly do things that other people just cannot do.

SOUTH AFRICA
V
CURTLY AMBROSE & COURTNEY WALSH

THE PROTAGONISTS

South Africa
Returning to Test cricket after 22 years. They were all making their debuts, except their captain, Kepler Wessels, who had played 24 Tests for Australia. They had never before played the West Indies.

Curtly Ambrose
(Leeward Islands & West Indies)
Aged 28. Playing his 34th Test, starting with 140 wickets.

Courtney Walsh
(Jamaica & West Indies)
Aged 29. Playing his 51st Test, starting with 174 wickets.

SOUTH AFRICA'S KEPLER WESSELS

CURTLY AMBROSE

COURTNEY WALSH

The defence of Fortress Barbados

One-off Test • Bridgetown • April 23, 1992

While the West Indies ruled world cricket in the 1980s, the South Africans believed they could have beaten them. Finally, the ban was lifted. Facing one another for the first time, South Africa needed only 79 runs to win with eight wickets in hand. What price West Indian invincibility now?

South Africa were back in the fold. And these were heady days. They returned to the international cricket scene after 32 years in the wilderness, re-entering with their first-ever matches against India – a one-day series in India. Then they had reached the semi-finals of the World Cup which followed soon afterwards, in a campaign which had seen them win their first match of any sort against the West Indies and also beat Australia

comprehensively. Now they were playing the first Test match of their comeback, on their first visit to the West Indies.

During the apartheid years, South Africans had been only too well aware of the power of the West Indian fast bowling machine sweeping all before it. With that power just beginning to dim, this was not at all a bad time for a first Test against them, in cricketing terms at least.

Politically the tour was inevitably going to attract attention – and, indeed, with the reform programme being put to the vote in South Africa only three weeks before their arrival in the Caribbean, the tour would have been in doubt had the electorate turned it down.

The very sight of a South African Airways 747 touching down in Kingston, Jamaica, was the signal of a new era.

Curtly Ambrose, Courtney Walsh and Richie Richardson lead the lap of honour after the victory over South Africa

SOUTH AFRICA				
BATTING	RUNS	H.O.	B	
1 RUSHMERE	3	C		7
2 HUDSON	163	B		9
3 WESSELS	59	C		7
4 KIRSTEN	11	C		9
5 CRONJE	5	C		6
6 KUIPER	34	C		11
7 RICHARDSON	8	C		16
8 SNELL				
9 PRINGLE				
10 DONALD				
11 BOSCH				

Historic moments: The two teams mingle for a group photo; Allan Donald bowls Keith Arthurton; the scoreboard shows Andrew Hudson's century – the first by a South African debutant; and ex-Aussie player Kepler Wessels becomes the first captain of South Africa to set foot on a cricket pitch in the West Indies

The first examination of the South African cricketers' credentials came swiftly. In front of packed crowds at Sabina Park and twice in Port-of-Spain, they discovered the reality of playing in the West Indies' back yard and lost the one-day series 3-0 and each match by a distance. If that was a huge disappointment to them after the World Cup, they now had the daunting task of a one-off Test match at Kensington Oval in Barbados, where the West Indies had not lost for 57 years.

The curiosity of seeing South Africa here should have ensured that the ground would be packed, but popular reaction to selection policy in this area can be somewhat parochial and Bajans were incensed at the omission of local boy Anderson Cummins. Under the catchy slogan "NO CUMMINS NO GOINGS", they stayed away and the match was played before a handful of spectators. It looked as if this might be signalling an inauspicious start for the new era in West Indian cricket. Richards, Greenidge, Dujon and Marshall were gone and a new man was in charge – Richie Richardson.

There is a theory in Barbados that the only life you are going to get out of the pitch will come on the first morning, and with that in mind Kepler Wessels put the West Indies in after winning the toss. But he then had to watch Desmond Haynes and Phil Simmons quickly run up 99 for the first wicket. They were past 200 with only three wickets down, until the West Indian batsmen generously contributed to their own downfall and the last seven wickets toppled for 43 runs. South Africa were replying to their 262 before the close.

By the end of the second day the vistors were only eight runs behind with six wickets in hand and Andrew Hudson 135 not out, having batted throughout to become the first South African to make a century on his Test debut. He went on to make 163, but the innings fell away as the lower order tried to attack Jimmy Adams' slow left-arm bowling. His four wickets restricted the lead to 83.

Before they could regain the lead, the West Indies had lost Simmons, Haynes and Richardson to Tertius Bosch and Richard Snell. After tea on this third day, Brian Lara

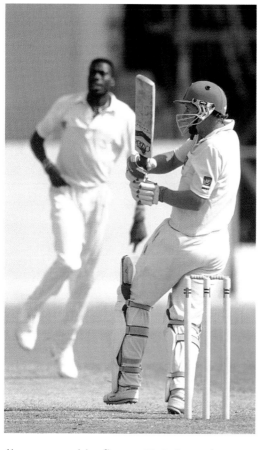

and Keith Arthurton added 52 for the fourth wicket, until Allan Donald produced the sheer speed to remove them both. He and Snell snatched one more wicket apiece before the close when, at 184 for 7, the West Indies' lead was a slender 101 and depending – not for the first time – on Jimmy Adams, who was 23 not out.

After the rest day Adams managed to coax another 99 runs out of the last three wickets. At least he had made sure that South Africa would have to score over 200 – if only just – and that gave the West Indian bowlers a chance.

It looked a very good chance when Ambrose had Hudson caught at slip second ball and then shot one under Mark Rushmere's bat to bowl him for 3. South Africa were 27 for 2 and the target of 201 wasn't looking quite so easy.

Kepler Wessels was joined now by another gritty fighter in Peter Kirsten and, after Ambrose, the rest of the

West Indies attack failed to live up to his fire. Determinedly the third-wicket partnership grafted their way to the close – by which time, at 122 for 2, they had just about sealed their victory for the next day. With eight wickets in hand, they would need only 79 more.

All round the world, cricketers who had found the West Indies such a handful over the years noted the inevitability of South Africa's success at the first attempt with a rueful smile.

Courtney Walsh had gone wicketless in the first innings, when Richardson had used him as the first change. He had come on as the second change in this innings – but he began proceedings on the final day and in his second over, with only one run added to the overnight score, he found the edge of Wessels' bat and Lara dived to his left at slip to take the catch. Wessels out for 74 and Kirsten was now joined by Hansie Cronje. In harness now

Mr Ambrose shows South Africa what they've been missing by bowling opener Mark Rushmere, but Andrew Hudson fights fire with fire during his innings of 163

Return of the hurricane

WEST INDIES v ZIMBABWE • 2000

History was to repeat itself eight years later, on March 20, 2000. Another African team was playing its first Test match in the Caribbean, and this one was threatening to impose an even greater humiliation. The West Indies were facing the prospect – indeed the likelihood – of defeat at the hands of cricket's minnows, Zimbabwe.

In Port-of-Spain, Trinidad, nine wickets for Heath Streak had dismissed the West Indies for 187 and 147, while Zimbabwe's wicketkeeper captain Andy Flower had made a hundred. On the last morning Zimbabwe were set a derisory target of 99 to win. The visitors looked certain to stroll to a crushing victory.

But Courtney Walsh, now aged 37, removed the dangerous Neil Johnson, Reon King had Trevor Gripper LBW, and suddenly Zimbabwe were 20 for 2 and experiencing the kind of uncertainty that had haunted so many first-time tourists to the Caribbean.

The door was ajar – and Franklyn Rose promptly kicked it down by destroying the Zimbabwean middle order. The 28-year-old Jamaican had been on medication for an injured foot, but he rose to the occasion now. Murray

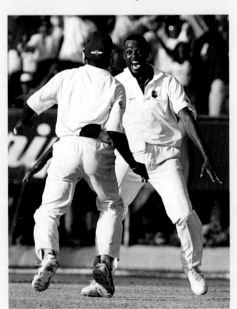

Courtney Walsh breaks Kapil Dev's record by claiming his 435th Test victim

Goodwin, Andy Flower and Stuart Carlisle were all caught behind and Streak LBW, raising only 16 runs between the four of them. Rose took 4 for 19.

Nor were the old warhorses, Walsh and Ambrose, to be denied – Walsh bowling Grant Flower, the only Zimbabwean to make double figures, for 26.

He finished with 2 for 18 while Ambrose mopped up three wickets for a typically miserly eight runs.

Zimbabwe were shattered and defeated by 35 runs – all out for 63. Yet again, when the chips were down, the Windies' pace quartet had simply blown their would-be conquerors away.

with Ambrose, Walsh was into full flight, despite bowling into the southerly breeze. Both bowlers were at full tilt, combining movement and speed and benefiting from some variations in bounce. The Jamaican and the Antiguan were bowling for Barbados' pride in the 57-year Kensington record of West Indies invincibility here.

Seven more runs were scratched out before Cronje

> '*Fast bowlers hunt in pairs, they say. Over the years Curtly and I have grown very close; we know what's best for each other and what's best for the team.*'
>
> COURTNEY WALSH, 'HEART OF THE LION'

nicked a ball from Ambrose to David Williams behind the wicket, to be out for 2. Walsh did the same to Adrian Kuiper before he had scored. Suddenly it was 131 for 5. Only nine runs had been added in the day, as three wickets had fallen and now the win that had looked like low-hanging fruit had been whisked away into the remote high branches.

Peter Kirsten was still there and encouraged Dave Richardson, his new partner, to accompany him through the 70 runs still needed. Kirsten battled his way to his half-century and they gathered another 11 runs together.

Now the target was only another 59 runs away. But then Walsh delivered possibly the decisive blow as he nipped one back in to Kirsten, found the inside edge of the bat and it clattered into the stumps. Kirsten bowled Walsh 52. It was 142 for 6.

Very soon it was 142 for 7 as Walsh immediately had Snell caught at short leg for a duck.

Walsh had blasted away South Africa's last realistic hope. Now it was over to Ambrose to mop up the tail, which operation he carried out with ruthless efficiency, bowling Pringle and then off successive balls having Richardson caught behind and bowling Donald. South Africa were all out for 148.

Ambrose had taken six for 34 and Walsh four for 31. Together they had blasted away South Africa's last eight wickets for the addition of 26 runs in an hour and forty minutes. To the South Africans' disbelief, the West Indies had won by 52 runs and it was still Fortress Barbados.

Joint Man of the Match Curtly Ambrose reaches out for victory

West Indies v South Africa

Kensington Oval, Bridgetown, Barbados
South Africa won the toss and fielded

18.4.1992 - 23.4.1992
West Indies won by 52 runs

West Indies	1st innings		2nd innings	
D.L.Haynes	c Wessels b Snell	58	c Richardson b Snell	23
P.V.Simmons	c Kirsten b Snell	35	c Kirsten b Bosch	3
B.C.Lara	c Richardson b Bosch	17	c Richardson b Donald	64
*R.B.Richardson	c Richardson b Snell	44	lbw b Snell	2
K.L.T.Arthurton	c Kuiper b Pringle	59	b Donald	22
J.C.Adams	b Donald	11	not out	79
+D.Williams	c Hudson b Donald	1	lbw b Snell	5
C.E.L.Ambrose	not out	6	c Richardson b Donald	6
K.C.G.Benjamin	b Snell	1	lbw b Donald	7
C.A.Walsh	b Pringle	6	c Richardson b Snell	13
B.P.Patterson	run out	0	b Bosch	11
Extras	(b-0, lb-7, w-0, nb-17)	24	(b-17, lb-11, w-0, nb-20)	48
TOTAL	(all out)	**262**	(all out)	**283**

Fall of Wickets	1-99	2-106	3-137	4-219	5-240
	6-241	7-250	8-255	9-262	10-262

Fall of Wickets	1-10	2-66	3-68	4-120	5-139
	6-164	7-174	8-196	9-221	10-283

Bowling Analysis	O	M	R	W	O	M	R	W
A.A.Donald	20	1	67	2	25	3	77	4
T.Bosch	15	2	43	1	24.3	7	61	2
R.P.Snell	18	3	83	4	16	1	74	4
M.W.Pringle	18.4	2	62	2	16	0	43	0

South Africa	1st innings		2nd innings	
M.W.Rushmere	c Lara b Ambrose	3	b Ambrose	3
A.C.Hudson	b Benjamin	163	c Lara b Ambrose	0
*K.C.Wessels	c Adams b Ambrose	59	c Lara b Walsh	74
P.N.Kirsten	c Lara b Benjamin	11	b Walsh	52
W.J.Cronje	c Lara b Adams	5	c Williams b Ambrose	2
A.P.Kuiper	c Williams b Patterson	34	c Williams b Walsh	0
+D.J.Richardson	c Ambrose b Adams	8	c Williams b Ambrose	2
R.P.Snell	run out	6	c Adams b Walsh	0
M.W.Pringle	c Walsh b Adams	15	b Ambrose	4
A.A.Donald	st. Williams b Adams	0	b Ambrose	0
T.Bosch	not out	5	not out	0
Extras	(b-4, lb-6, w-1, nb-25)	36	(b-4, lb-3, w-0, nb-4)	11
TOTAL	(all out)	**345**	(all out)	**148**

Fall of Wickets	1-14	2-139	3-168	4-187	5-279
	6-293	7-312	8-316	9-336	10-345

Fall of Wickets	1-0	2-27	3-123	4-130	5-131
	6-142	7-142	8-147	9-148	10-148

Bowling Analysis	O	M	R	W	O	M	R	W
C.E.L.Ambrose	36	19	47	2	24.4	7	34	6
B.P.Patterson	23	4	79	1	7	1	26	0
C.A.Walsh	27	7	71	0	22	10	31	4
K.C.G.Benjamin	25	3	87	2	9	2	21	0
K.L.T.Arthurton	3	0	8	0				
J.C.Adams	21.4	5	43	4	5	0	16	0
P.V.Simmons	5	1	13	0				

Umpires: D.M.Archer, S.A.Bucknor

Man of the Match: C.E.L.Ambrose & A.C.Hudson

NASSER HUSSAIN'S ANALYSIS

'The rest of world cricket would have breathed a sigh of relief'

'I can imagine all the Caribbean players gelling together to take on a team of white South Africans.'

The West Indies had several factors in their favour here. First, it was at Barbados – and, not having been beaten there for 57 years, they had a record they were determined to uphold. The longer a record like that endures, the harder you fight to preserve it.

Secondly, there was their pride. People were accusing them of losing it and they wanted to disprove that.

And then they were playing South Africa, almost within days of apartheid finally being overturned. Now it cannot be denied that, at that time, the West Indies team used the African element of their background as part of their team-building. They used to get a bit of stick about it in some islands, because there is actually a wide mix of races in that area. On some

occasions Guyana has been almost like a home game for us with the crowd not wanting the West Indies to win. But in a cricket match you use anything to try to get your team up for it, whether it be right or wrong, and I can imagine all the Caribbean players gelling together to take on a team of white South Africans.

In 1992 the Walsh and Ambrose combination was in its prime and bowling extremely quickly. It was only two winters before this that Jack Russell and Robin Smith almost got us to safety in the Test match at Barbados and then Ambrose rolled us over by taking eight for 45. A few months after this Test against South Africa, he took seven for 1 against the Aussies in an astonishing spell at Perth. Ambrose is not just a destructive

NASSER HUSSAIN'S ANALYSIS

'Ambrose is not just a destructive bowler – he never, ever gives you anything to hit.'

bowler – he never, ever gives you anything to hit. In my whole career I've only hit him for only four or five boundaries, even when I've got a century against the West Indies.

I love touring the West Indies because it is an electrifying atmosphere. When you first go in to bat, you hear the roar, you see Ambrose looming at the end of his run, then the fielders come crowding in on you, all about 6ft 5 tall … it's an overwhelming experience. You have to get used to it quickly or you'll soon be in trouble.

Against high-quality fast bowling such as the West Indies, wickets fall in clusters. When you're in, they sit back and set a ring field and appear to go through the motions. But they get one wicket and the crowd go up and suddenly it's back to four slips and two gulleys, and the whole

atmosphere is different. One minute everything seems to be going quite well. The next minute, you're in the middle of a collapse and there's nothing you can do about it.

It's a feeling that all the Test-playing countries had come to know only too well in the Eighties – but this would have been the first time the South Africans had experienced it.

The rest of world cricket would have breathed a sigh of relief that South Africa weren't able to just stroll back into the Test arena and immediately beat the all-conquering West Indies who had lorded it over the rest of us for so long.

The Springboks would have loved that – the Windies defending a 57-year record at Barbados and they just pop in there for a one-off Test and beat them. So for once I'm glad that Curtly and Courtney did the business.

And another one bites the dust… Ambrose bowls Meyrick Pringle and it's nearly all over for South Africa. Opposite: A trophy stump that means more to Curtly than most

CRICKET'S GREATEST BATTLES

GRAHAM GOOCH
V
CURTLY AMBROSE

THE PROTAGONISTS

Graham Gooch
(Essex & England)
Aged 37. Playing his
87th Test – his 15th
as captain, having
previously made 6,548
runs, with 14 centuries.
Would go on to
become England's
leading run-scorer.

Curtly Ambrose
(Leeward Islands
& West Indies)
Aged 27. 6'7" tall fast
bowler from Antigua,
playing his 29th Test,
having taken 112
wickets.

GRAHAM GOOCH

CURTLY AMBROSE

Captain Gooch's revenge

First Test • Headingley • June 8 & 9, 1991

*Graham Gooch had a score to settle. Eighteen months earlier, England had threatened
to pull off a sensational series win in the Caribbean – before the captain's own injury
and the fast-bowling genius of Curtly Ambrose pulled the rug from under their feet.
But Headingley was not the venue Gooch would have chosen for a rematch…*

The broad shoulders of Graham Gooch did sometimes seem as if they were carrying the whole
weight of the England team. Never was this more
the case than in this Headingley Test. Fresh in his mind
was a 2-1 defeat in the Caribbean which might easily have
gone the other way – but England had faltered after Gooch

got injured, and Ambrose had cashed in with 20 wickets in
the last three games. Gooch took that sort of reversal hard
and was determined to redress it.

Headingley was not a very popular ground with the
England team. Pitches here had a history of being, in the
opinion of many of them, not altogether fit for Test

cricket. They had, however, produced some exciting Tests in typically English conditions. Clouds come over north Leeds and the ball swings, while the pitch maintains the life so suited to English seamers. That, though, would not disappoint a West Indian attack of Ambrose, Walsh, Patterson and Marshall.

In these conditions, Viv Richards inevitably put England in to bat. It was a first day interrupted by rain and bad light, and batting was not easy. England had two new batsmen – Graeme Hick, who was given a hostile welcome to Test cricket and took eleven overs to make 6, and Mark Ramprakash, whose 27 looked assured enough to impress onlookers. But England were all out early on the second day for 198.

England's third debutant was Glamorgan's seam and swing bowler Steve Watkin, who made the first breakthrough by having Desmond Haynes caught behind for 7. But the wicket that electrified the ground was the run-out of Carl Hooper by a lightning-reaction direct throw from Ramprakash at cover. This young man was an exciting prospect.

On the second afternoon, England's steady seam attack used the conditions well to whittle away at the West Indies. Only the great Richards defied them, launching into his Glamorgan teammate, Watkin, to be 73 not out at the close, when the West Indies were eight wickets down.

Graham Gooch hooks during his epic innings of 154 not out, which gave him the upper hand over opposing skipper Viv Richards

Next morning he fell to Derek Pringle in the first over and twenty minutes later the West Indies were all out for 173 – 25 runs behind.

So, half an hour into the third day, Graham Gooch and Michael Atherton came out to open England's second innings. Little over an hour later, any hopes of capitalising on that slender lead looked dashed. Atherton, Hick and Lamb had all been sent back by the brooding, vengeful figure of Curtly Ambrose. England were 38 for 3, of which Gooch had 29, and Ramprakash was coming in on a hat-trick. He survived it and the pair made it through to lunch at 47 for 2.

The West Indies were denied a wicket through the middle session of the day, too. Gooch was all concentration and fierce determination. He eliminated all loose shots, judging what he could leave alone with perfection. The unprofitability of bowling short at him encouraged the West Indies bowlers to give him a fuller length, enabling some more shots to be played. Three-quarters of an hour before tea he reached his fifty, made out of England's 80 for 3.

Ambrose struck again straight after tea. Ramprakash had batted two hours and 20 minutes for 27 before he was caught behind by the diving Dujon. The fourth-wicket partnership had added 78 – crucial runs in a low-scoring match. Next ball, though, the West Indies were in the ascendant, as Robin Smith was LBW. It was 116 for 5. England were only 141 ahead and Ambrose, with all five wickets, was on a hat-trick again. This time it was Jack Russell who denied him.

But Ambrose had a head of steam up. Though he could not break through the stern, moustachioed England captain, he managed a sixth wicket when Russell edged to the 'keeper and England were 124 for 6.

Gooch and his Essex colleague, Derek

Curtly Ambrose celebrates trapping Robin Smith LBW for a second-innings duck

Pringle, had only another 25 minutes before rain ended the day. It was 143 for 6. The lead was 168 and Graham Gooch was 82 not out. Curtly Ambrose had striven mightily and had been rewarded with six wickets. But the wicket he most wanted had eluded him. Gooch was still there.

On the fourth morning, Gooch and Pringle added 17 in the first half-hour, but were then driven off by rain, which held up play for a further half-hour. Rain continued to threaten and just as it was about to bring them off again, Gooch clipped Walsh away for his twelfth four to reach his hundred. In doing so he became only the fourth man to have made a Test century on each of England's six Test grounds. He had been batting for almost five-and-a-half hours but, with England taking an early lunch at 183 for 6, he knew there was still work to do. The lead was 208.

It was 240 when the new ball was taken in the afternoon session and the third over with it accounted for Pringle, caught behind off Marshall for 27 – his contribution to a decisive seventh-wicket stand of 98, of which Gooch had made 61.

The new ball needed changing when it was only seven overs old and the replacement seemed to suit Walsh and Marshall, who quickly removed Phil DeFreitas and Watkin. Now Gooch's batting partner was Devon Malcolm. He manoeuvred the strike to add another 14 runs to the total before the inevitability of Malcolm having his stumps scattered by Marshall. England were all out for 252.

Graham Gooch had carried his bat through the completed innings for 154 not out. His seven-and-a-half hours at the crease had been persistently interrupted by breaks for rain and bad light, but he had kept his concentration for 331 balls, 18 of which he had hit for four. He was only the second Englishman to carry his bat through an innings in England in 111 years of Test cricket in the country. What was more important to him was that with a lead of 277, he had given England a good chance of victory.

It was as if Gooch's innings had inspired the side. DeFreitas ran in for the first ball of the West Indies' second innings, Phil Simmons went to cut – and played on. But there was little more that evening as the rain returned. They were 11 for 1 and would need 267 more on the last day.

Haynes and Richie Richardson added another fifty in the morning before Pringle had Haynes caught off bat and pad and then Watkin picked up three prize wickets in three overs – including Viv Richards. Suddenly it was 88 for 5.

After lunch the obdurate Jeffrey Dujon helped Richardson add 48, but then DeFreitas struck again, accounting for both of them. The final slide was rapid, the last five wickets falling in half an hour. The West Indies were all out for 162 and England had won by 115 runs.

Gooch would go on to make 480 runs in the series, which would be tied two-all, and Ambrose would take 28 wickets, but for both of them this Headingley Test would be their outstanding performance.

England v West Indies

Headingley, Leeds, England
West Indies won the toss and fielded

6.6.1991 - 10.6.1991
England won by 115 runs

England	1st innings		2nd innings	
*G.A.Gooch	c Dujon b Marshall	34	not out	154
M.A.Atherton	b Patterson	2	c Dujon b Ambrose	6
G.A.Hick	c Dujon b Walsh	6	b Ambrose	6
A.J.Lamb	c Hooper b Marshall	11	c Hooper b Ambrose	0
M.R.Ramprakash	c Hooper b Marshall	27	c Dujon b Ambrose	27
R.A.Smith	run out	54	lbw b Ambrose	0
+R.C.Russell	lbw b Patterson	5	c Dujon b Ambrose	4
D.R.Pringle	c Logie b Patterson	16	c Dujon b Marshall	27
P.A.J.DeFreitas	c Simmons b Ambrose	15	lbw b Walsh	3
S.L.Watkin	b Ambrose	2	c Hooper b Marshall	0
D.E.Malcolm	not out	5	b Marshall	4
Extras	(b-0, lb-5, w-2, nb-14)	21	(b-4, lb-9, w-1, nb-7)	21
TOTAL	(all out)	198	(all out)	252

Fall of Wickets	1-13	2-45	3-45	4-64	5-129	1-22	2-38	3-38	4-116	5-116
	6-149	7-154	8-177	9-181	10-198	6-124	7-222	8-236	9-238	10-252

Bowling Analysis	O	M	R	W	O	M	R	W
C.E.L.Ambrose	26	8	49	2	28	6	52	6
B.P.Patterson	26.2	8	67	3	15	1	52	0
C.A.Walsh	14	7	31	1	30	5	61	1
M.D.Marshall	13	4	46	3	25	4	58	3
C.L.Hooper	4	1	11	0				
I.V.A.Richards	4	1	5	0				

West Indies	1st innings		2nd innings	
P.V.Simmons	c Ramprakash b DeFreitas	38	b DeFreitas	0
D.L.Haynes	c Russell b Watkin	7	c Smith b Pringle	19
R.B.Richardson	run out	29	c Lamb b DeFreitas	68
C.L.Hooper	run out	0	c Lamb b Watkin	5
*I.V.A.Richards	c Lamb b Pringle	73	c Gooch b Watkin	3
A.L.Logie	c Lamb b DeFreitas	6	c Gooch b Watkin	3
+P.J.L.Dujon	c Ramprakash b Watkin	6	lbw b DeFreitas	33
M.D.Marshall	c Hick b Pringle	0	lbw b Pringle	1
C.E.L.Ambrose	c Hick b DeFreitas	0	c Pringle b DeFreitas	14
C.A.Walsh	c Gooch b DeFreitas	3	c Atherton b Malcolm	9
B.P.Patterson	not out	5	not out	0
Extras	(b-0, lb-1, w-0, nb-5)	6	(b-0, lb-1, w-0, nb-6)	7
TOTAL	(all out)	173	(all out)	162

Fall of Wickets	1-36	2-54	3-58	4-102	5-139	1-0	2-61	3-77	4-85	5-88
	6-156	7-160	8-165	9-167	10-173	6-136	7-137	8-139	9-162	10-162

Bowling Analysis	O	M	R	W	O	M	R	W
D.E.Malcolm	14	0	69	0	6.4	0	26	1
P.A.J.DeFreitas	17.1	5	34	4	21	4	59	4
S.L.Watkin	14	2	55	2	7	0	38	3
D.R.Pringle	9	3	14	2	22	6	38	2

Umpires: H.D.Bird, D.R.Shepherd   **Man of the Match:** G.A.Gooch

NASSER HUSSAIN'S ANALYSIS

'Headingley was his first chance to take Curtly on again'

'The next morning I was amazed to see Gooch in the nets working with his coach, Alan Lilley, because there was something not quite right in this seven-hour innings of 154 not out that he wanted to sort out!'

Ambrose, Walsh, Patterson and Marshall – not a bad attack on that up-and-down Headingley pitch. The main thing I remember about that game is the next morning, as I drove to Chelmsford, hearing people all over the country talking on the radio about what a magnificent innings it was. I dropped into the Essex County Ground to check my post and was amazed to see Gooch in the nets working with his coach Alan Lilley on the artificial surface, because there was something not quite right in this seven-hour innings of 154 not out that he wanted to sort out!

That summed up Graham Gooch at that time. Anyone else would have said: "I've done it, I'll enjoy my moment of triumph and put my feet up for a week." Some people would view it as tinkering too much. But that is why Gooch was a phenomenal player. For a spell of five or six years he had an utter dedication to batting, and to English cricket. Every time you saw him he was either training or working on his batting.

He wasn't limited in the way that even great players such as Gower and Boycott were. He was the master of the explosive innings, with so many one-day records – 198 not out in a B&H Cup match, the most runs ever in the Sunday League, NatWest and B&H Cup, the most Gold Awards ... But when the chips were down, he could defend and survive and grind out a match-winning innings on an unpredictable wicket like Headingley against the best attack in the world.

He also had an immense mental capacity for batting. I remember towards the end of his career, the last game of the season, Essex versus Derbyshire. Both teams were mid-table with nothing much to play for, and in the second innings he thumped about 180. It was the last first-class innings of that summer and it just showed the mental capacity of the bloke that he could still do that in a game where we would probably either have come 11th or 10th.

If you have that sort of dedication all the time then, when you get into situations like the Test match at Headingley, that's when all the practice and the mental toughness pay off.

I didn't really know him when he was young, but the story at Essex is that he wasn't a big trainer. He was a flair

NASSER HUSSAIN'S ANALYSIS

'Gooch wasn't limited in the way that even great players such as Gower and Boycott were. He was the master of the explosive innings … but when the chips were down, he could defend and survive against the best attack in the world.'

Richie Richardson and Jeff Dujon wait in vain for Gooch to slip up

'When Gooch became
captain of England,
he decided he had to
lead from the front:
The team need me…'

*'He needed to
change things
in order to keep
himself fresh,
in the same way
that a golfer is
constantly
tinkering with
his swing.'*

player who would just lift that heavy Grey-Nicholls bat in the air and try to hammer runs as quickly as possible. Then halfway through his career he decided to become more of a technician and bat for long periods of time. He needed to change things in order to keep himself fresh, in the same way that a golfer is constantly tinkering with his swing.

When he became captain of England, he decided he had to lead from the front: "The team need me." In the West Indies in 1989/90, when he broke his finger, it was a great loss to the side not having him there at the top of the order. From being in a position where we nearly led 2-0 in the series, we slumped to a 2-1 defeat – and Ambrose

was the main destroyer, with 20 wickets in the last three Tests. It was a very bitter blow.

That's one reason why Gooch was so determined to do well when the West Indies came to England. The other was that his desire to match himself against the best opposition. He used to say: "I like facing Curtly because he's the best test of my abilities" – which I always found amusing and slightly mad.

Leeds was his first chance to take Ambrose on after that Caribbean tour, and you could have predicted that it would be a real battle of the giants between two blokes who were probably the leading batsman and bowler in the world at that time. So I'm pleased the Essex lad came out on top.

NASSER HUSSAIN'S ANALYSIS

'Gooch used to say: "I like facing Curtly because he's the best test of my abilities" – which I always found amusing and slightly mad.'

Gooch in his pomp, taking the battle to the West Indies

Photographic Acknowledgements

The photographs for the book have been supplied mainly by Allsport and Patrick Eagar Photography.
Thanks to Rob Harborne and Ian Kirkpatrick at Allsport, and Phil Burnham-Richards at Hulton Getty;
and to Patrick, Lynda Cole and Jan Traylen at Patrick Eagar.
Thanks are also due to Helen Dobson at Corbis,
to David Frith for his Brian Close 'bruises' shot,
to Roger Mann for his help and photographs, especially on 'Bodyline',
and to Graham Morris and Diana Morris for supplying the photographs
for 'Gatting v Shakoor Rana'.